MW00777711

HOW TO
MAKE MONEY
IN
LISTED OPTIONS

HOW TO
MAKE MONEY
IN
LISTED OPTIONS

by

LIN TSO

Veteran Securities Analyst
and
Author of Four Investment Books

A World of Books That Fill a Need

Frederick Fell Publishers, Inc., New York

Library of Congress Cataloging in Publication Data

Tso, Lin, security analyst.
  How to make money in listed options.

    1. Stocks. 2. Put and call transactions. I. Ti-
tle. II. Title: Listed options.
HG6041.T76   332.6'45   75-45112
ISBN 0-8119-0265-X

Copyright © 1976 by Lin Tso

For information address:

Frederick Fell Publishers, Inc.
386 Park Avenue South
New York, N.Y. 10016

Published simultaneously in Canada by:
George J. McLeod, Limited
73 Bathurst Street
Toronto 2B, Ontario

MANUFACTURED IN THE UNITED STATES OF AMERICA

DEDICATION

Once Again, As Always,

To My Dearest Sou Cheng

For Her Love, Devotion, and Unbounded Help

CONTENTS

x.

xvii.

INTRODUCTION

The new investment world of listed options is both exploding and worth exploring for every serious investor.

In little more than two years since its advent, the listed options market has grown by leaps and bounds and is expected by many to dwarf even the Big Board in just a few years.

The rapidly gaining popularity of listed options is understandable. For one thing, this new highly versatile investment medium provides a means of making money regardless of the market direction—up, flat, or down—if you know how to make use of it. For another, listed options have great appeal to speculative and conservative investors alike.

For speculative investors, listed options provide a means of achieving leverage to a degree never before attainable. Sometimes options can go up several hundred percent in just a matter of weeks. Naturally, leverage works both ways. It can magnify your loss on the downside as much as it can magnify your gain on the upside. Moreover, options can expire worthless, meaning a total loss of your money. You need not, of course, ride options all the way down, since a highly liquid secondary option market should enable you to get out with only a limited loss.

For the more conservative investor, listed options provide a low-risk means of obtaining higher yields without significantly increasing portfolio exposure. Now investors can generate additional premium income by writing options on the core stocks of their portfolios that they mean to hold anyway. Listed options are believed to be the only investment medium where one could start with a gain instead of a loss!

The rate of return on an options portfolio could considerably exceed that on a straight debt, equity, or mixed portfolio. According to one estimate, every million dollars committed to the regular writing of call options on a diversified list of stocks should produce $250,000—minus commissions and portfolio losses, plus the dividends.

Whether you invest conservatively or speculatively—or somewhere between—you should learn about the uses, the strategies, the opportunities, and the risks of the versatile listed option.

This book is essentially a "method" book designed to give the reader a comprehensive, practical coverage of the many-faceted possibilities of the listed option market. Particular stress is placed on the varying forms and combinations of "writing" and "buying" techniques of listed options, and on the multiplying applications of "spreading" strategies.

To illustrate "writing," "buying," "spreading," and other hedging techniques, "laboratory" or "worksheet" methods are used to help the reader understand the intricacies of option hedging characteristics and their major possibilities. To simplify calculations in "case" studies, dividends, commissions, and other transaction costs generally are disregarded despite their importance.

It cannot be overemphasized here that application of any of the formulas, methods, or techniques sampled in this book should be made *only on a basis fully reflecting commissions, interest expenses, dividends, and other considera-*

tions that have a direct bearing on the costs of a transaction; otherwise, a calculated profit actually may prove to be a loss. Readers are advised to consult their own brokers for such transaction costs.

It is my earnest hope that this book will provide a one-volume reference library on a subject that hitherto has been little known and much misunderstood. It should prove useful to investors of substantial means, to traders, brokers, and students of options, as well as to average serious investors seeking either above-average returns and/or leveraged profits with predetermined risks.

I wish to express my heartfelt thanks to a number of individuals who offered valuable suggestions. I am particularly indebted to Leon Pomerance, James J. Horan, Richard Jo Brignoli, Jerry Goldsmith, Martin Presler, Kenneth L. Marsh, Warren H. Bree, and Martha J. Ogborn.

Lin Tso
New York City

HOW TO
MAKE MONEY
IN
LISTED OPTIONS

CHAPTER I

OPTIONS: WHAT—WHY—HOW

What Is an Option?

What is an option?

Webster's New World Dictionary gives the following definitions of "option":

1. A choosing; choice.
2. The right or liberty of choosing.
3. Something that is or can be chosen.
4. The right to buy or sell something at a fixed price.

Cost of Insurance

Options have been used in Europe for more than three centuries. For instance, when a grower of tulip bulbs was worried about the safe arrival of a shipment he had contracted to deliver, he would buy an "option," as insurance, from another grower on an equivalent amount of the merchandise at the prevailing price.

The "option" would cost him a relatively small amount of money, as insurance, against a possibly costly breach of contract.

A Rather Common Instrument

Options are used extensively both in individual and

business existence today. An option is a rather common instrument in innumerable areas.

When you buy an automobile, for instance, you have a choice to buy many accessories, such as power brakes, power steering, etc., that are termed "optional"; that is, "elective," or at your choice. When you buy a house, for another instance, an increasing number of items, such as fireplace, dishwasher, basement, etc., have become "optional."

It is interesting to note here that the price paid for options traded both on the national exchanges and over the counter is called the "premium," the same term used in the insurance business as the cost of buying insurance to protect one's life, house, automobile, etc.

No Mystique

It is strange that stock options should have acquired the mystique that they have. As an individual you must have gone through many instances involving options or their equivalents.

Instead of Irrevocable Commitment

Before you decide to buy a particular house, for instance, you may need a little time to think it over instead of making an instantaneous, irrevocable commitment.

To avoid a possibly costly decision and yet, at the same time, not let somebody else grab the house away from you, you may place a binder" of, say, $100 or so that would give you a period of a week, or even a month, to make your decision. Such a "binder," essentially, constitutes an "option" on the house.

Limited, Instead of Costly, Loss

As another example, an option is a particularly important instrument for a real estate developer seeking to assemble a sizable plot on which to build a large apartment house or an office building, especially if the project would involve "buying out" a number of small lots that would be indispensable to his required large plot of ground.

Instead of risking a very costly failure, the developer would buy an "option," for a relatively small consideration, on each of the small lots. In the event that he is unable to obtain options on all property segments, he could abandon the project, with his loss limited to the cost of the options acquired.

Property Options

Such options on property normally are composed of three important items: (1) a description of the property to be acquired, (2) the price at which the property may be acquired, and (3) the time period during which the buyer must exercise, or lose his right to acquire.

If the option-holder selects not to exercise his purchase rights during the option period, the option expires. The option writer (the property owner) keeps the option money regardless of whether the option is exercised.

Stock Options

Similarly, a stock option contract has three basic ingredients: (1) a description of the item the option buyer may purchase from the seller (writer) of the option, (2) the price at which the item may be purchased or sold, and (3) the time period during which the buyer must exercise, or lose his right to purchase.

For the rights granted by the option, the option buyer pays and the option writer (seller) receives a certain amount of money. The option writer will keep the option money whether or not the option is exercised.

Three Basic Ingredients

In the case of listed options, each option is for 100 shares of a specific, widely held, actively traded security. In option parlance, this security is known as the "underlying security."

The price at which the option buyer may purchase the stock from the option writer is the "striking price" or the "exercise price."

The expiration date is the last day on which the option buyer is entitled to exercise his option to purchase the security. All listed options are assigned three months apart, expiration dates covering periods up to nine months

Varying Combinations

For a given stock, with its options listed on one of the national exchanges, there may be trading, at the same time, in as many as three options with the same or different striking prices but different expiration dates.

Liquid Market

Since options have long been available on the over-the-counter market and have not made much headway, what has made the two-plus-year-old listed options market explode across the country in such a short span of time? One simple answer: liquidity.

This liquidity comes from the creation of a centralized ready market made possible by the standardization of option contracts for listed options.

Standardized Contracts

For one thing, by contrast to the standardized expiration dates of listed options, over-the-counter options can expire on any business day of the year.

For another, an infinite variety of exercise, or striking, prices exists for over-the-counter options. In listed options, on the other hand, striking prices are, as a rule, fixed at 5-point, 10-point, 20-point, and 25-point intervals.

WHY PEOPLE BUY OPTIONS

Buying call options offers many investors an attractive combination of a potentially large profit from a relatively small investment, with a known and predetermined risk.

Example: Investor A bought 100 shares of XYZ at $45 per share, at a total cost of $4,500.
Investor B bought a call option on 100 shares of XYZ at $45 per share, for $300 as the cost of the call option.

Here are the obvious advantages for Investor B over Investor A:

1. Higher Leverage
    If XYZ rises from $45 to $65 per share, Investor A will have a profit of $2,000, amounting to a 44.4-percent return on his investment of $4,500.
    On the other hand, Investor B will have a profit of $1,700 ($2,000 minus $300 as cost of the option), amounting to a 567-percent return on his much smaller investment of $300.

2. Limited and Predetermined Risk
    If XYZ declines from $45 to $25 per share, Investor A will lose $2,000 or 44.4 percent on his $4,500 investment, while Investor B's loss will be limited to $300.
    In fact, Investor B knows in advance that the most he

can lose is the price of $300 he has paid for the option. While relatively modest in absolute amount, the loss of $300 would constitute a 100-percent loss of Investor B's option capital. On the other hand, theoretically, Investor A could lose the entire $4,500 if XYZ went down to zero.

Investor A, however, has a major advantage over Investor B: while Investor B would have no recourse after the expiration of his option, Investor A could always hold on to his stock for possible eventual recovery.

WHY PEOPLE SELL OPTIONS

Writing (selling) call options offers investors an opportunity to increase, sometimes significantly, the income derived from their investments. Also, option writing enables investors to reduce substantially the costs of their securities.

Example: if you presently own 100 shares of Xerox at $70 per share, you might consider writing one October 70 option for $750.

Twofold Advantages

The advantages in doing this are twofold:

First, you receive an immediate cash flow of $750 to work with right now.

Secondly, the $750 in option premium has the effect of reducing your investment in 100 shares of Xerox from $7,000 to $6,250, amounting to a 10.7-percent cost reduction.

Cost Reduction and Downside Protection

This same $750, or 10.7-percent cost reduction, also

will provide you with that amount of protection on the downside; meaning that if Xerox declines 7½ points, or 10.7 percent, from the price level at which you bought the stock, you still would break even.

However, if Xerox should remain unchanged at expiration, the option would expire worthless and the $750 option premium would, in effect, constitute an increase in the overall return on capital.

Drawbacks and Limitations

Investors would do well to remember the drawbacks and limitations inherent in options, which should be carefully weighed against the potential rewards.

For option sellers (writers), for instance, they would give up almost all of the benefits of a possible further advance in the price of the underlying stock, in return for the option premium received.

For option buyers, the premium they paid for the right (option) to buy the underlying stock at a specified price within a specific period of time would become a total loss of their money if the option should expire worthless.

A majority of option investors appear to believe that more money has been made on the writing (selling) side than on the buying side, meaning, actually, that more money has been lost on the buying side than on the writing (selling) side.

CHAPTER II

LISTED OPTION MARKET

Exchange Traded Option Market

While trading in options is nothing new, what is new is the emergence of an active, organized market as a result of trading in listed call options on four national exchanges— the first two being the Chicago Board Options Exchange (CBOE) and the American Stock Exchange (AMEX).

The securities industry marked the beginning of a new era on April 26, 1973, when the CBOE began its trading in call options on a limited number of New York Stock Exchange stocks. The list of such stocks has been steadily expanded.

Explosive Growth

Growth on the CBOE has run far beyond anyone's expectations. In slightly more than two years the CBOE has become the second-largest place for securities business in the United States, in terms of shares represented by the options, next only to the New York Stock Exchange. Even with only 66 underlying stocks presently listed on the CBOE, daily volume is running at a level not too far from one-third of that of the New York Stock Exchange. The CBOE plans to bring the total to 100 by year's end.

Other indications of the magnitude of growth in listed options trading on the national exchanges are the following statistics: on the Amex during May 1975, 265,747 options were received to buy 26,574,700 underlying shares listed on the New York Stock Exchange. This was 24.2 percent higher than in April and more than double the February total, the first full month of Amex options trading. Indicative of the extensive public participation in options trading is that the public was said to have generated 67 percent of the record May volume.

Emerging Major Investment Vehicle

Not since the height of the growth-stock craze of the late 1960s has Wall Street displayed such mass enthusiasm as its euphoria over options trading.

According to Amex chairman Paul Kolton, there was no question that "only a small portion of the potential universe for options trading has been tapped at this point." The most commonly heard estimate is that only 5 percent of active brokerage-house clients have so far engaged in options trading.

Conceivably, listed options will emerge as a major investment vehicle of the '70s comparable to what the mutual fund was in the '50s and '60s.

Impact on Stock Markets

It is uncertain at this point whether the markets for the underlying securities are being affected by options trading.

Most observers point to one financial sector they feel is being hurt by the interest in options—the secondary market for low-priced, lower-quality stocks.

Since one may participate in the market action of such Blue Chip stocks as Exxon with an option that costs less than $10, even speculators would be hesitant to speculate on low-quality, low-priced stocks.

Fundamental Versus Trading Role

The great appeal of listed options to a broadening public market is understandable. For one thing, the formation of the national-exchange-traded options markets has created a new investment tool that can be employed by aggressive and conservative investors alike. For another, the existence of a continual auction market has immeasurably enhanced the liquidity of both option buyers and option sellers (writers).

Aggressive investors, by buying an option, can participate in the market at minimal cost and with high leverage. Specifically, those who want to gain a foothold in today's market without exposing their whole flank may do so by buying an option on 100 shares of stock on the premise that the stock may rise in value. If the stock fails to perform as expected, their maximum loss is the option premium.

For conservative investors, options are used as a capital-protection, rather than speculative, tool because of their hedging characteristics that can limit risks. Specifically those who own stock and want to hedge their position may grant an option on that stock, promising to sell it at a given price by a given date if called upon to do so. The premium they receive from the buyer may be viewed as an additional yield on their investment, or as a cushion against its decline in value.

Thus options can play a more fundamental role than merely as a trading vehicle.

Basic Option Strategies

To explain options in the simplest way: If you believe the price of the stock will increase, you buy a call option. On the other hand, if you believe the price of the stock will stand still or decline, but you still want to hold the stock, you sell a call option.

An ever-growing number of options are bought as hedges against existing positions. Call option purchase can guarantee a purchase price against a short position. Conversely call option writing (selling) can often guarantee a sale price against a long position.

There are a multiplicity of reasons to sell (write) a call option or to buy a call option. Thus buying or selling pressures can create relative price variances between options with various striking price and expiration dates.

While the basic option strategies are simple, their applications are limited only by human imagination.

Possible Combinations

When you consider the possible combinations of striking prices and expiration dates, you can see there can be many different options traded on one underlying stock.

In combination with positions in other securities, options can produce portfolio configurations with risk/reward possibilities that are not obtainable in other media of investment.

For instance, it is possible to hedge against price changes by means of protective hedging, which uses a combination of stocks and calls or a combination of buying and selling calls. For another instance, you can establish aggressive spread and hedge positions, with limited risk, which are designed to take advantage either of market swings or movements in the market or price changes in a particular security.

Indicative of the growth potential of option-oriented portfolios is the rapid growth of option funds. Actually, new hedged funds have been created to invest only in the options market. Listed options funds enjoy strong merchandising appeal because of their arbitrage characteristics.

The spectacular growth of the listed options market is indicated by the fact that, even in the initial months of its existence, the CBOE's average daily volume on a very small number of stocks exceeded that of the over-the-counter option market.

Basic Concepts

While the listed options market is radically different, especially structurally, from the over-the-counter options market, strategies involving the use of options for both the buyer and the writer remain essentially the same.

Despite differences in terms of the contracts in different option markets, none will likely change the basic concepts of option contracts underlined by their three inherent possibilities: capital-protection possibilities, income-producing possibilities, and trading possibilities.

Underlying such profit-making possibilities are the almost timeless arbitrage and hedging methods that are utilized to attain capital-protection and income-generating possibilities, as well as to maximize trading possibilities to profit from market movements in any direction.

ARBITRAGE

Exploiting Price Differential

Essentially arbitrage is accomplished by an offsetting transaction in two securities or in a related security of the same company. Specifically, arbitrage involves almost simultaneous purchase and sale of the same security, or substantially identical securities, in different markets in order to profit from a price differential.

By means of convertible securities, arbitrage seeks to cash in on profits resulting from price differential regardless of the direction of the general market or of underlying stocks.

Relative Versus Absolute Price Relationships

Determination of likely relative price relationships between convertible securities is easier than forecasting the absolute price of the underlying securities. Generally, conventional investing methods are aimed at forecasting the absolute price some time in the future. As opposed to conventional investing, arbitrage is not dependent upon such variables as disappointing earnings, compression of P/E multiples despite increased earnings, etc.

Objective Mathematical Approach

The analysis of convertible securities lends itself to an objective mathematical approach far more successful than conventional investment techniques. In the last analysis, arbitrage is a mathematical investment method that can, by varying and combining a number of basic techniques, be made to design a hedged portfolio that will profit within a range of rising, stable, and falling prices.

Arbitrage has long been a significant and steady source of income to many New York Stock Exchange member firms and other professional investors. It has been particularly profitable during periods of market weakness where other investment areas have been moribund. Generally, Wall Street professionals have performed arbitrage activities primarily for their own accounts because of the difficulty of finding enough situations to satisfy external demand.

Broadened Arbitrage Opportunities

The growth of listed options has considerably broadened arbitrage opportunities.

Just as other arbitrage methods, option technique involves identifying options that are either underpriced or overpriced relative to the price of the underlying security. The overvalued option is sold short against the purchase of the undervalued option.

MAJOR INNOVATIONS

Continuous Auction Market

One of the major innovations brought to call options trading by the national exchanges has been the creation of a continuous auction market in standardized option contracts, in which holders and writers may liquidate their positions as easily and as simply as other securities listed on major stock exchanges.

As opposed to the standardized expiration dates of listed options, OTC options can expire on any one of the business days of the year. An infinite variety of strike prices exists for OTC option contracts.

Secondary-Market-Making Ability

Perhaps the single most important feature of listed options is the option writer's ability to liquidate his position when and if desired. This makes possible a whole array of defensive and aggressive techniques that was never available in the OTC options market.

The national options exchanges provide for the resale of options through their secondary-market-making ability. Instead of being merely an inert derivative of the market in the underlying stock, listed options have developed into a kinetic instrument with a market value of its own.

On the other hand, there is little liquidity or secondary-market-making ability for OTC call option writers until the expiration of options contracts or until option buyers see fit to exercise the options.

Commodity Futures Concept and Strategies

To begin with, the CBOE borrowed the futures concept of delivery months from the commodity market.

Also, the CBOE has successfully applied most of the key commodity strategies to the options market. Essentially the CBOE is a commodity exchange using options on stocks as opposed to commodity futures.

Quality List

While options are available at only a fraction of the price of their underlying securities, they provide a low-cost participation in quality stocks due to the stringent listing requirements on both the CBOE and the Amex.

The listing requirements on the CBOE are even more stringent than on the nation's major stock exchanges. These strict requirements help supply the options writer with a quality list from which to select.

Eligibility Standards

To have its options eligible for listing on the CBOE, the underlying security must meet certain requirements, including (1) a minimum of 10 million outstanding shares, of which 80 percent are held by the general public; (2) a minimum of 10,000 stockholders; and (3) a minimum price of $10 per share at the time of approval for listing.

In addition, the issuing corporations of the underlying securities (1) must have earned a minimum $500,000 per year in operating profits after taxes for the five years preceding the listing; (2) must not have been in default on its obligations during the past ten years; and (3) must have earned all dividends paid on all classes of securities for the five years preceding the listing.

The Amex maintains stringest listing requirements identical to those of the CBOE with respect both to earning and dividend-paying capabilities and to other basic characteristics.

With regard to earning and dividend-paying power, issuing corporations of the underlying securities (1) must have had a net income, after taxes but before extraordinary items net of tax effect, of at least $500,000 for each of the previous five years; (2) must have not defaulted on its obligations during the past ten years; and (3) must have earned in each of the last five fiscal years any dividends (including the fair market value of any stock dividends) paid in each such year on all classes of securities.

Broad Distribution

To assure that the underlying securities of listed options are widely held and actively traded, the Amex requires that the underlying securities must have (1) a minimum of 10 million outstanding shares of which at least 80 percent are held by public stockholders; (2) a minimum of 10,000 holders; (3) a minimum one-million-shares trading volume per year in each of the two preceding calendar years; and (4) a minimum of $10 per share in market value.

Unique Guarantor Function

Both the CBOE and the Amex are served by a central Options Clearing Corporation that performs a unique role in options trading.

Immediately after sales and purchase orders are matched and executed, there remains no connection between the purchaser and the seller. The Options Clearing Corporation assumes the obligation and becomes the purchaser to the seller and seller to the purchaser. It guarantees all options transactions that clear through it, assuring the purchaser that the stock will be delivered, and the seller that he will be paid.

"Certificateless" Securities

Options are called "certificateless" securities because customarily no certificates are issued to evidence ownership of exchange-traded options. The customer's position is evidenced by the confirmations and periodic statements that customers receive from their brokers.

Despite the rapid volume growth, markets have been orderly and technical foul-ups few. High-volume trading in certificateless securities has been achieved, and option transactions clear in one day, compared with five days for stock clearing.

Virtually Unlimited Uses

Despite the growing popularity of trading in listed options, only a comparatively small number of investors have begun to realize its many-faceted possibilities.

This little-known, much-misunderstood investment tool has virtually unlimited uses for investors knowledgeable about options.

Probably the most versatile investment vehicle of the '70s, listed options are found to have multiplying applications limited only by imagination. Some of them are quite conservative. Others are more speculative. Listed options sometimes act as insurance policies to lock-in profits, sometimes as high-leveraged means of maximizing profitability, sometimes as hedges to contain losses from other risk transactions.

For Traders and Institutions

For traders, the use of listed options opens up a whole new range of leverage and hedging possibilities.

For institutional and other substantial investors, listed options have opened up new avenues for seeking above-average return, as well as capital protection through writing call options.

For hedgers, listed options provide a varying combination of long, short, straddle, and spread strategies to maximize profit making.

Beginning of Institutional Participation

Listed options are especially important and timely now that a recent ruling by the Comptroller of the Currency permits national bank trust departments to deal in covered call options.

So far, institutions are participating on a relatively small scale. They account for an estimated 5 to 10 percent of volume, compared with 4 or 5 percent a year ago.

Most major banks have set up an internal monitoring unit to experiment with their own funds, mostly from pension funds. Several banks have taken a more aggressive stance by marketing option writing to customers.

Current Limitations

Banks are limited by almost built-in factors. For one thing, at the present time they can not buy options except to close out a position. For another, they are prohibited from buying stock expressly for the purpose of selling options. They are not allowed to sell short. They can only use a "one-on-one" writing technique.

Present and Pending Legislation

Under present law, tax-exempt institutions—profit-sharing and pension funds, for example—are subject to taxes on income from writing options. Such institutions are waiting for tax-law changes to permit liberalization of tax treatment.

A Treasury-backed bill is pending in Congress to free option income from taxes, just like income from dividends, interest, and capital gains for these institutions.

Specifically, for some time there has been a bill in the House of Representatives that would establish statutorily that premiums derived from option writing are not subject to the tax on "unrelated business income" that tax-exempt organizations must pay on other than specified categories of income. The House Ways and Means Committee has tentatively approved a provision that would remove impediments to option writing by tax-exempt organizations.

Incorporation of the above provision into a general tax revision bill before Congress would open up a whole new cadre of option writing prospects.

CHAPTER III

CHARACTERISTICS OF LISTED OPTIONS

Exclusive Characteristics

The listed call option is a new instrument of investment with exclusive characteristics and features.

A listed call option is defined as a contract given for an agreed premium, entitling the buyer or holder, at his option, to buy on or before a fixed date, 100 shares of a specific, widely held, actively traded security at a predetermined price.

The security is known as the underlying security. The price at which the option buyer may purchase the stock from the writer of the option is the exercise or striking price.

Basic Ingredients

Essentially a listed call option has three basic ingredients, namely, the specific security the option buyer may purchase from the seller or writer of the option; the price at which the security may be purchased (or sold); and the time period during which the buyer must exercise or lose his right to purchase.

Time Period

The time period during which the option buyer must

exercise or lose his right to purchase amounts to the life of an option.

The price that the option buyer pays for that right to buy or not to buy the underlying security generally is in recognition of the time value placed upon the option's upside profit potential and limited downside risk.

Time Value

An option is a wasting asset, its value diminishing with time and completely vanishing on expiration date.

Everything else being equal, the longer the life remaining in an option, the larger the premium. Conversely, the shorter the life remaining in an option, the smaller the premium. For example, everything else being equal, a three-month option is invariably cheaper than a six-month option.

The life of a conventional (over-the-counter) option may be whatever buyer and seller mutually agree. By and large, however, such options are granted for periods ranging between 30 days and one year.

On the other hand, listed options have only three clearly defined time periods: namely three months, six months, and nine months.

Standardized Expiration Months

During the first two years of listed options trading on national exchanges, listed options were assigned one of four standardized expiration dates: the last business Monday of either January, April, July, or October.

The expiration date is the last day on which the buyer or holder is entitled to exercise his option.

Starting with mid-year 1975, additional expiration months of February, May, August, and November have been phased in to avoid overcrowding with the gradual addition of new listed options.

47

Short-Life Warrant

With a liquid secondary market, a listed call option essentially is a short-life warrant. The main differences between such an option and a warrant are that:

1. A listed call option is relatively close to expiration, as its longest possible maturity is only nine months.
2. Listed calls are issued by option writers while warrants are issued by companies.

Perpetual Regeneration

A listed call option has a major advantage over a warrant in that the former enjoys a perpetual regeneration of new warrants at new strikes and new expiration dates.

It has been the practice of the national options exchanges to issue a new series of option contracts for the same underlying security when a substantial price change occurs in that security.

Unlike the stock markets, where each stock has a fixed number of shares that can be traded, there is no predetermined number of options. It depends solely on the number sellers are willing to write and buyers are willing to buy.

Striking Prices

Listed call options can be traded with the same expiration date, but different striking prices.

Striking prices are as a rule fixed at five-point intervals for securities trading below 50, ten-point intervals for securities trading between 50 and 100; and 20-point intervals for securities trading over 100.

With regard to over-the-counter options, the striking price is automatically reduced on the ex-dividend date, by the exact value of any dividends, rights, or stock distributed to shareholders.

On the other hand, the striking price of listed options will not be reduced by cash dividends but will reflect all other distributions. Cash dividends on the "long" stock position accrue to the option writer because exercise prices on the CBOE and the Amex are not reduced by such dividends.

Compelling Mathematics

Since an option sells at a percentage of the price of the underlying security, small price changes in the price of the underlying security can result in large percentage changes in the price of the option.

From the standpoint of both writer and buyer, the mathematics of listed options are compelling.

The option writer obtains additional income from his portfolio, while at the same time reducing his risk. The premium received from option writing can be considered as a partial hedge against a possible decline in the price of the stock. The buyer maximizes the number of shares to be controlled with minimum cost.

OPTION PREMIUM

The key to option trading is the amount of money a buyer pays to a seller or writer for the right to buy 100 shares of a given stock within a certain time limit. The writer of the option keeps the premium whether or not the option is exercised.

Cost of Option

The cost of an option is called the "premium." This is payable at purchase of the option and is not applicable to the purchase price of the stock at exercise of the option.

The premium, however, does become part of the cost

basis of your stock if you should exercise your option.

General Yardsticks

While there is no precise formula for calculating the amount of premium, there are some general yardsticks:

The amount of the premium varies with the market price and volatility of the underlying stock, as well as with its time duration and striking price.

Other factors influencing the size of the premium include market trends, the cost of money, and the level of general interest or lack of interest in options.

Supply and Demand Factors

Essentially the premium is a reflection of supply and demand.

In times of generally rising stock prices, there is less interest in writing call options but more interest in buying them. This tends to raise the level of option premiums.

Conversely, in times of generally weak or declining stock prices, there is greater interest in writing call options but less interest in buying them. Premiums thus tend to decline.

Also, price levels of underlying securities play a role in determining premiums.

Volatility

A major premium-influencing factor is the volatility of the underlying security.

As a general rule, with a traditionally volatile stock, its option is likely to command a higher premium than the option for a stock that normally trades in narrow price limits. Apparently a stock that fluctuates widely presents more risk to the option writer, therefore a greater chance for the option buyer to exercise the option profitably.

Premium Cost of Short- and Long-Term Options

Percentagewise, the largest premium is often paid for the shortest period of time.

The increment of premium for the period between the nearest expiration date and the next longest usually is significantly less than the premium for the first three months.

An option on a stock selling for $20 per share usually costs, percentagewise, more than an option on a stock selling for $60.

As a rule of thumb, 90-day call options range from 8 percent to 12 percent of the market price of the stock. Six-month options run from 10 to 16 percent, or higher in the case of very volatile stocks.

Premium Components

With a liquid secondary options market, the price of the option can be considered as having three components: intrinsic or tangible worth, discounted potential appreciation, and premium. Premium, in this sense, means that portion of the option price the buyer pays in excess of intrinsic worth.

During a call option's life, the option will usually sell at a premium—meaning more than the option's tangible worth. The size of the premium essentially reflects the option's upside leverage and limited downside risk.

Generally, a larger premium will be paid for an option providing greater upside leverage coupled with greater downside risk protection than for one of equal life with less upside leverage and less downside protection.

Normally an option will command a price in excess of its actual tangible worth. The amount option buyers are willing to pay over an option's tangible worth is called "premium" in the narrow sense of the term. Option buyers are willing to pay such a premium in the expectation that the underlying security will rise and the option will develop more value.

Mathematic Relationship at Expiration
At expiration, the option price will reflect itself directly in terms of its mathematical relationship to the underlying security. In other words, the only remaining value of an option "at expiration" will be its tangible value. This is the amount—if any—that the exercise price of the option is below the current market value of the underlying security.

Three Basic Price Relationships
When traded on the national exchanges, listed options maintain three basic price relationships with the underlying security, namely: options "at market," options "in the money," and options "out of the money."

"At Market" Options
"At market" options are options whose striking prices are equal to the market value of the underlying stock.

When one sells an option "at market" against a long position, one is usually seeking above-average return. Generally the writer of options "at market" believes that his annual return will, on average, be greater than he could realize by being long on common stocks.

"In the Money" Options
"In the money" options are options whose striking prices are below the current market price of the underlying stock.

Thus, options with their striking prices below the market price are said to have tangible worth or intrinsic value. This "in the money" is in addition to value for time remaining.

One would sell these options if one were generally short-term bearish on the market. Another important factor motivating such option writing is the desire to increase overall return by selling options against stocks held in one's portfolio.

"Out of the Money" Options

"Out of the money" options are options whose strike prices are above the market value of the underlying stock.

Options with their strike prices above the market value of the underlying stock are said to have no tangible worth. This does not mean, however, that the call will not command a value. Usually it is only at or very near to an option's expiration date that it will not maintain a premium.

For a call without any tangible worth, the entire price that the option sells for constitutes its premium.

Since there is an optimistic bias in "out of the money" options, it would make sense to buy stocks and sell "out of the money" options if you believe the stocks you are buying are not going to change very much in price. However, when you buy such a stock be sure that you would like to own it anyhow, and if the price of the security goes up you are willing either to surrender the stock or close out the call.

For an investor who owns the stock, an "out of the money" option can be used to maximize potential return and, at the same time, derive some income from his "long" position.

CHAPTER IV

ANALYSIS OF CALL OPTIONS

Most Popular Form of Options

Of all kinds of options, the call option is by far the most popular form, accounting for the great majority of all option transactions.

Essentially a call option purchaser anticipates an increase in the value of the underlying security by investing a fraction of the cost of the stock as a means of obtaining greater leverage on his investment.

Probably the single most important attraction of purchasing call options is leverage. In essence, leverage means the possibility of very large percentage gains on the predetermined premium risk within very short time periods.

Speculative Opportunities

Since options may be purchased for only a fraction of the underlying stock's market value, they provide attractive vehicles for speculation.

Opportunities include those for day-to-day trading by aggressive investors. Often a price move of several points in the underlying security can produce 40-percent or more gain in the option in a single day. A significant number of options have doubled or more in one session.

Predetermined Risk

Leverage runs either way, however. A large number of

options have declined more than 50 percent in one trading session.

Offsetting the risk, however, is the assurance to the purchaser, who knows in advance exactly how much he can lose—namely his premium, no matter how far the underlying stock may decline. Call option buyers are only risking the cost of the call, which is considerably less than the price of the stock. In other words, call buyers stand to profit from any appreciation in the price of the stock, while knowing at all times exactly how much they can lose.

Alternate Courses

Buying an option is an alternate course to investing in the underlying security. There are many instances where it is less risky and less expensive to control shares of XYZ with an option than it is to go long on the stock, either outright or with margin.

The key to determining these alternate vehicles lies in weighing the risk-reward parameters and the leverage factor of the option.

Leverage Factor

(1) Relative to cash purchase: As a rule of thumb, for the same amount of money involved in an outright acquisition of 100 shares of stock, you can control far more shares through the use of calls.

(2) Relative to margin purchase: Buyers of a call option achieve great leverage by establishing a position in a selected stock several times larger than a margin position (based on the current 50-percent margin).

Magnification Factor

The magnifying effect of potential option profitability is indicated by the following comparison:

Consider the case of two investors who are impressed with the future prospects of the same stock, each of whom has about $5,000 in investable cash. Assume that Mr. A decides to buy 200 shares of the stock at $50 and margin his purchase. Under current margin requirements he puts up 50 percent of the market value, or $5,000. Also assume that Mr. B buys ten calls (1,000 shares) at the strike price of $50, for a premium of $500 per call, or $5,000.

Now, suppose the stock moves to $75 within the next six months, Mr. A, who bought 200 shares on margin, would have a profit of $5,000 ($15,000 less the $5,000 debit in his margin account and less $5,000 initial investment). On the other hand, Mr. B could exercise his ten calls at $50 and immediately sell the 1,000 shares at $75, thereby realizing a profit of $20,000 ($25,000 less the $5,000 he paid for the ten calls).

Reward Parameters

For the same amount of cash outlay, Mr. B would gain $20,000 from his ten calls, or 400 percent on his money.

Mr. A, however, would gain $5,000, or only 100 percent on this investment. The relative leverage between Mr. B and Mr. A is 4 to 1.

Near-Term Movements

Thus, the buyer's side of an option contract is where the leverage lies and, consequently, where the big profits are. For a fraction of the price of the underlying stock, the option buyer can speculate on the stock's near-term movements.

Risk of Total Loss

Leverage can operate in reverse, of course. At the worst, options could result in total loss of premium money in a relatively short period of time.

It happens when the underlying shares fail to reach the striking price before the option runs out. If options are not exercised before expiration, they lose all value.

In the preceding examples, Mr. B could lose his entire $5,000 if the stock were to become worthless. On the other hand, Mr. A could hold on to his stock for possible recovery, since total erosion of stock value is highly unlikely, though theoretically possible, because the underlying stocks, as a result of the strict listing requirements by the national options exchanges, are generally of blue-chip quality.

Need Not Ride All Way Down

The option buyer need not, however, ride all the way down, because of the existence of a continuous listed options market. He can limit his loss just as he can in the stock market.

A rule of thumb calls for an option buyer to consider getting out while he still has 75 percent of his premium money intact.

Resale Market

The ability to resell listed options at any time on the national exchanges serves to limit option losses and to realize profits with less stock price movement than in the OTC market.

On the other hand in the over-the-counter options market, it is extremely difficult to sell a call option with the market price below the strike price. An over-the-counter option holder can rarely, if ever, obtain any reasonable value for the time remaining in his option contract.

Salvage Value

There is an exception to the general rule of cutting loss with about 75 percent of the option premium still intact: it probably would pay for the option holder to hang on once an option had dropped below 2 ($200 per option), especially if it had three weeks or more to run.

The fact is that an option selling for 175 or so represents a small salvage value, and frequently such low-priced options could double in price in the last few weeks.

Maximum Leverage With Minimum Risk

Well-selected low-priced options represent the maximum leverage with minimum risk. Low-priced call options primarily mean call options in the 1½ to 2 range that would be most advantageously purchased at the beginning of a time period.

Assume that XYZ is available at 19 with the possibility that it may rise to 25. Assume that an intermediate call at the striking price of 20 is available at 1¼ or 1⅜.

If you buy that call option at the start of the time period, there is not much that will erode its value except time.

As a general rule such low-priced options more often than not hold their premiums almost to expiration date. Even if the stock goes to 18, for the next month, it won't lose more than a quarter of a point. And on the upside it has far greater potential.

Cushion Factor

It is possible that there will be a cushion factor at work that tends to support the price of a listed option as it descends.

The same cushion factor has been indicated in the behavior of commodity futures markets, from which the listed options market drew several of its basic elements.

In a number of key commodity markets, the premium widens when commodity prices decline, then narrows again when commodity prices recover. The closer commodity prices get to their floor, the more pronounced the effect of the floor becomes. The premium is a reflection of the value commodity futures traders place on the limited risk.

Striking Resemblance

There is a striking resemblance between commodity futures and listed call options. Just as with commodity futures, listed options have a predetermined downside risk.

It stands to reason, therefore, that if a listed option still has a meaningful period of exercisable life remaining, it tends to develop into an increasingly attractive candidate for purchase as its price descends, simply on the basis that its potential loss is becoming progressively smaller even if its possible gains are highly speculative.

Relative Percentage Moves

The degree of upside leverage an option provides is dependent upon the actual movement of the underlying security.

In order to ascertain the rate at which a call option will appreciate relative to the percentage advance of its underlying security, one must project a specific stock move. Dividing the resulting percentage move of the call option by the projected percentage move of the underlying security gives us the potential leverage an option offers.

One formula calls for option purchases only when the purchaser envisions a price move in the underlying security of approximately three times the premium at risk.

Option-to-Double Formula

To determine the percentage move required for the call price to double to maturity we divide the sum of twice the option's cost plus the exercise price by the price of the underlying stock per formula below:

$$\text{Required \% move for call to double at maturity} = \frac{2(OP) + SP}{MP}$$

OP—Option Premium
MP—Market Price
SP—Exercise Price

Option-to-Breakeven Formula

For an option buyer to break even at maturity, it will be necessary for the call's intrinsic value at expiration to equal the option's cost.

To determine the percentage of the underlying stock advance required for a call option buyer to break even, we divide the price of the call plus its exercise price by the price of the underlying stock per formula below:

$$\text{Option Breakeven} = \frac{OP + SP}{MP}$$

OP—Option Premium
MP—Market Price
SP—Exercise Price

Option-to-Become-Worthless Formulas

The following two formulas are used to measure the extent of stock decline before an option becomes worthless at expiration

60

1. Formula A—for call options with positive intrinsic value.

   To determine the percentage by which the underlying stock must decline to make the call worthless at expiration, we divide the option's intrinsic value by the price of the underlying stock, as follows:

   $$\text{Formula A} = \frac{\text{P.I.V.}}{\text{MP}}$$

   P.I.V.—Positive Intrinsic Value
   MP—Market Price

2. Formula B—for call options with negative intrinsic value.

   To determine the percentage the underlying security must decline to make the call worthless at expiration, we divide the negative intrinsic value by the price of the underlying stock, as follows:

   $$\text{Formula B} = \frac{\text{N.I.V.}}{\text{MP}}$$

   N.I.V.—Negative Intrinsic Value
   MP—Market Price

Intrinsic Value

The intrinsic value of a call option is the difference between the market value of the underlying security and the striking price of the option.

A call option is said to be "in the money" when its striking price is below the market value of the underlying security. A call option is said to be "out of the money" when its striking price is above the market price of the underlying security.

Relative Leverage and Risk

The greatest leverage is usually obtained with the "out of the money" option and the least with the "in the money" option.

On the other hand, purchasers of "out of the money" options stand a greater chance of losing all of the funds invested than buyers of "in the money" options.

In assessing the relative risk of "in the money" and "out of the money" options, the total amount of dollar exposure per option must be weighed.

The existence of both "in the money" options and "out of the money" options has considerably broadened investment opportunities.

"IN THE MONEY" OPTION TECHNIQUES

A significant number of "in the money" option buying techniques are available to sophisticated investors.

Technique #1—High-Leveraged Call Options

Illustrative of the technique of buying high-leveraged call options is the following example:

Since on April 21, 1975, the July 60 option on Union Carbide (NYSE-63 ⅛-UK) was in the money 3⅛ points, its price at 6 indicated an actual cost of 2⅞, which was a fairly inexpensive way of controlling a

$60-plus stock in a dynamic uptrend. An advance of 2⅞ points, or only 4.5 percent, from the current market level would enable the July 60 option to move point for point with the common. Despite flat unit sales, UK was benefiting from higher prices in all areas. Current P/E ratio of 7 was less than half its 10-year average P/E of 13.5.

Two weeks later, as UK had moved 3¼ points or 5 percent from 63⅛ to 66⅜ on May 5, 1975, its July 60 option had jumped 50 percent from 6 to 9, indicating the dynamics of high-leveraged calls.

Investors who had bought the original call could either take a quick 50-percent (before commissions) profit or venture for further possible gains.

Technique #2—Low-Cost Dynamic Call Options

A low-cost, dynamic, "in the money" call option was available on May 5, 1975, on the October 25 call option on International Harvester (NYSE-28½-HR). Since the option was "in the money" 3½ points, its price at 5⅛ indicated an actual cost of 1⅝ which was an attractive six-month-plus call on a recession-resistant growth stock. HR is a leader in agricultural equipment business that was in an uptrend despite the recession. Technically, it had achieved a breakthrough at 27, with an upward objective of 32–34. Estimated 1975 earnings of $6.00 indicated a P/E of 4.8 versus its 12-year average P/E of 11. A 6.0-percent yield on indicated dividends of $1.70.

Technique #3—"Parity" Call Options

A one-point increase or decrease in the underlying

stock price usually results only in a fraction of a point movement in option premium. However, once an option reaches parity (the premium plus the exercise price equals the price of the stock), the premium is likely to move point for point with the stock.

Illustrative of "parity" options was the July 15 option on International Telephone & Telegraph (NYSE-20½-ITT) which on April 21, 1975, was available at 5¾ against the common stock price of 20½.

After two weeks, on May 5, 1975, the common had advanced 1⅜ points, or 6.7 percent, from 20½ to 21⅞, while the July option had moved 1⅛ points or 20 percent from 5¾ to 6⅞. The option advance was in line with the generally close-to-one-point-for-point movement with the common.

ITT's prospects seem to have improved, especially with possible expanding opportunities for telecommunications equipment. Technical trend now bullish.

Thus, if you consider the purchase of the underlying security of these "parity" options you may find it more attractive to buy the option instead. The difference in capital could be placed in high-yield instruments.

Short Options at Parity

Just as advantage was taken of July and October options available at slightly above parity or their intrinsic value, so consideration should be given to closing out option writing positions that were established at much lower levels, if the short option were selling near parity.

By closing out the position rather than waiting to exercise it, the writer would realize his gain as well as generate possible favorable tax consequences.

Technique #4—*Conservative Hedging Call Options*

Conservative hedge writers should consider writing "in the money" options for both maximum downside protection and high returns.

One illustration of the above conservative hedging technique was the July 40 option on Alcoa (NYSE-46-AA) on May 20, 1975.

With the July option 6 points "in the money," an actual premium of 1⅞ was available on the nine weeks remaining in the option.

This conservatively capitalized company, producing about half of the United States' aluminum cans, primarily used for soft drinks, is recession-resistant and, sometimes, even countercyclical.

Based on lower 1975 earnings of $4.25 (vs. $5.14 in 1974), current P/E was 10.8.

Technique #5—*"No Premium" Call Options*

Illustrative of the technique of buying call options at no premium was possible purchase on January 21, 1975, of the April 15 option of International Telephone & Telegraph then quoted at 16¾.

With the April 15 option selling at 1 15/16, the option purchaser would pay a ³/₁₆ premium based on the stock price of 16¾.

Lack of premium for buying a call option is probably due to an excess of option writers over option buyers.

Since the striking price of 15 is below the stock price of 16¾ the April 15 option was said to be "in the money." "In the money" options normally are more expensive to buy due to their intrinsic value.

Also illustrative of "no premium" call options was possible purchase of the July 20 option on June 12, 1975, on International Telephone & Telegraph which was quoted at 22⅞ on that date.

With the July 20 option available at 2⅞, it indicated zero cost on the option as the stock was 2⅞ points in the money.

Technique #6—"Discount" Call Options

Probably one of the best risk-reduction and profit-maximizing option techniques is to buy discount instead of premium.

Availability of buying an option at discount is most probably due to an excess of option writers over option buyers.

Some of "deep in the money" options are available at discount. Illustrative of the "discount option" buying technique was possible purchase on June 12, 1975, of the July 30 option at 13¼ of General Motors (NYSE-43⅜-GM) which was trading at a ⅛-point discount, as follows:

GM Common 43⅜
GM April 30 Option:
      Exercise price.................30
      Premium 13¼

                                 43¼

Discount......................................⅛

Readers should be aware, however, that such discount purchases are seldom available.

Deep in the Money

Option premiums generally more closely approximate intrinsic value as the option becomes deeper in the money and rise above intrinsic value as the underlying security declines toward the strike price.

CHAPTER V

CALL OPTION BUYING STRATEGIES

Essential Objectives

Long considered highly speculative, listed option buying is today offering a significant number of applications ranging from conservative to speculative.

Purchasers of listed call options generally have three principal objectives, namely, (1) leveraged participation with limited capital; (2) short-term trading; and (3) insurance.

From the above three primary objectives sophisticated investors have developed varying and derivative applications. Important among such applications are trading the option itself as a futures contract and hedging a profitable long stock position by selling a call option on that stock.

OPTION BUYING APPLICATIONS

1. Call Speculators

As a participation vehicle, option buying can be an alternative to the purchase of stock. In addition to their leverage factor, call options limit downside exposure to the cost of calls.

Illustrative of listed call options as a speculative alternative to purchasing the underlying security itself were possible buying on April 21, 1975, of either or both the July 15 option and the October 15 option of Tesoro Petroleum (NYSE-16-TSO).

TSO was one of the few oil producers looking for higher 1975 earnings per share than 1974's. Also bullish was the expected rise to 700 million tons of coal reserves under lease or option by mid-year. TSO had a strong base forming at 13½–15. Its 1974 high was close to 29. Current P/E ratio was a low 3.

Both the July 15 option at 2¾ and the October 15 option at 3⅝ were attractive. For an extra $87, the October 15 option for an additional three months was preferred. For less aggressive accounts, an alternate course was to buy the stock and then wait until it reaches the 20 level before writing options to gain higher option premium.

A month later, on May 20, 1975, TSO had advanced 3⅝ or 22.6 percent from 16 to 19⅝ while the July 15 option had jumped 82 percent from 2¾ to 5 and the October 15 option 70 percent from 3⅜ to 5¾.

Investors who had taken the above option positions could either take 82 percent and 70 percent (before commissions) profit respectively, on the July 15 option and October 15 option, or venture for further possible gains since TSO continued to be statistically cheap. Its fundamental position had been strengthened by its successful take-over bid for Commonwealth Oil.

Another illustration of call speculation was possible purchase on May 5, 1975, of the October 30 call option of Kresge (NYSE-28⅞-KG).

At a cost of 3⅞, KG's October 30 call option had considerable speculative appeal. Fundamentally, its year-ahead prospects remained strong despite expected lower earnings. Technically, the recent upside breakout on increased volume was highly favorable for further advance. With support at 24–26, the price objectives for KG were indicated at 31–33 for near term.

2. Limited-Risk Method

This approach can be described as "buying options and investing the difference." The technique provides an opportunity to benefit from a stock-price rise while protecting the investor against an adverse price movement.

The limited-risk technique involves purchasing call options on the same number of shares of stock that would otherwise have been bought outright and investing the balance in some short-term fixed-income securities.

The following illustrates this technique: on June 12, 1975, you decided to take a 100-share position in Syntex (NYSE-39¾-SYN).

Instead of buying 100 shares of Syntex for $3,975, you decided to take a far more limited risk by purchasing an October 40 call for 5⅛ that, for a 3-month-plus period, would enable you to participate in the possible rise of the stock.

Meanwhile, since you have used only part of the fund that otherwise would be required to buy 100 shares of Syntex, you invested the balance, amounting to $3,462, in some short-term fixed-income securities.

3. Establish a Position in Advance of Funds

One may buy a call option as a means of nailing down the price of a stock one intends to buy six or nine months later. One primary use of this "buy now, pay later" method is to establish a position in a stock in advance of an expected inflow of money.

Assume that Homestake Mining (NYSE-52¾-HM) appeared attractive to you on June 12, 1975, for possible recovery in the price of gold.

Assume that you would not have the funds to buy HM until late October.

In order not to miss a possible resurgence of gold prices, you bought an October 50 call for 7⅝, indicating a premium of 4⅞ points since the October 50 call was 2¾ points in the money. The October 50 call option had the effect of guaranteeing you, through its exercise, a definitive price until the option expires next October.

If, as expected, HM rises to 60, you can exercise your option and acquire 100 shares of HM at $50 per share.

4. Lock Up Profits

Many traders have gained handsomely since January of 1975 in the generally upward market but are unaware that they can lock up their profits and thus protect against a sudden market reversal.

Assume that in January you bought a July 50 call option of Digital Equipment (NYSE-DEC) at 8, which six months later was quoted at 97 on June 12, 1975. With the July 50 option trading at 49⅜, you have appreciated more than 600 percent on the option premium. It's time to take protective steps.

If you still believe DEC will continue to advance in price, you should sell the option at 49⅜ and use part of the proceeds to buy a new October 100 option at a cost of 11 points. Now, with a profit of $3,837 safely locked up (the difference between $4,937 from sale of the July 50 option and $1,100 as cost of the new October 100 option), you can afford to speculate on possible further rise in the stock.

Probably two of the most important listed option buying strategies are the use of listed options as a trading vehicle and as a hedge against a short sale.

71

5. Trading-Against Method

For a growing number of professional investors, one of the most important reasons for buying options is to use options to trade against. The ability to use a listed option to trade against can be quite profitable to the holder, especially in a "trading market," one that would fluctuate wildly.

A listed option contract is operable until it expires or is exercised. A trade or trades against an option do not nullify the option contract.

The holder of a listed call option may trade (short the stock) against the option. So long as one's original call option remains intact, one could trade repeatedly against the option until its expiration.

During the life of a listed option, its holder could trade many times against an option, sometimes to as many as ten trades during a six-month period.

(A) Trading Under Protective Umbrella

Such trades are made under the protective umbrella of the option and with the holder's risk predetermined.

Each time a trade is made, that trade is fully protected against unlimited loss if the trader's judgment should be wrong.

The number of opportunities to make trades against an option is limited only by the fluctuation of the stock and the trader's ability to judge the stock's movements.

(B) Trading in No-Trend Markets

When there is no definitive trend in stock prices, options can be used as a limited, instead of a full-fledged, commitment. Such options allow a certain

72

measure of participation before the market gives a clearer indication of its direction.

Thus, regardless of what happens to the price of the underlying stock, the holder's maximum risk in any long call option position is the total price of the option premium.

For example, instead of buying XYZ at 50, you buy a 3-month call with a striking price of 50 at a premium cost of $300.

If XYZ rises to 60, your call will gain in value and can be exercised at a profit.

If XYZ declines to 40, your loss will be limited to the premium cost of $300 instead of the $1,000 you would have lost had you bought the stock at 50.

If, when your call expires, the stock is still depressed, you could purchase another call if you feel it should recover a good portion of its decline.

(C) *Trading for Short-Term Movements*

Assume that you paid $300 for a 3-month call on XYZ with a striking price of 50. If XYZ rises to 60, you could sell it short and lock in a $1,000 gain.

Should the stock continue to advance, you could exercise your call to cover the short sale. If XYZ, instead, fell back to 55, you could cover your short sale by buying the stock, while continuing to be in a position to profit through the use of your call. If the stock advanced once more to 60, you could repeat the operation.

Through continuous trading of a security against an option, the investor is in a position to benefit from short-term reactions to a basic trend of the security, especially when an initial profit has been insured.

6. Hedge Against Short Sale

You may hedge the risk you have assumed in a short sale by buying a call option.

You can protect your short sales with a call because the option increases in value as the stock goes up. Your risk is limited to the costs involved in buying the option.

The alternative would be running the risk of having to cover a short sale at a higher price—and perhaps incurring a very substantial loss.

Should the market go against you, the call can be exercised to cover the short position. If the stock declines, the call can be allowed to expire, leaving a profitable short position.

As an example, you feel XYZ is overvalued at $60 and decide to sell short. In order to protect yourself, you buy a call at the same price. If the stock declines, say to $50, you buy 100 shares at that level to cover your short position, and take a 10-point profit less the cost of your call, which you allow to expire.

If the stock rises, you will be able to exercise your call in order to cover your short position.

Not Necessarily "Unison" Movements

It will very rarely be possible to sell short at the exact striking price of the listed option. The differential between the short-sale price and the striking price may be positive or negative and must be considered in addition to the call premium when evaluating the cost of the hedge.

In the above, we assume that the price of a listed call option and that of its underlying stock will move up and down in unison. In fact, since the two are traded in different markets and on different exchanges, they indicate movements not exactly in unison between the listed option and the underlying stock.

Among other important listed call option buying strategies are the following:

7. *Control More Stock With Same Money*

Because the price of an option usually accounts for a small percentage of the value of the underlying security, one can control a large amount of stock with a relatively small amount of money.

A rule of thumb is that a call option buyer controls about five to ten times the stock he could normally control with the same available capital. The same amount of money required to margin 100 shares of stock probably could be used to buy five calls.

8. *Release Cash While Maintaining Market Position*

Through a listed call option one may release one's funds by selling the stock while still maintaining control over the same number of shares during the life of the option.

9. *Buy at Below-Market Price*

Under certain conditions a stock can be acquired through its options at less than the cost of the underlying security, especially if the stock has a low dividend yield.

10. *Acquire Option at No Cost*

Suppose you buy stock and a call at the same time.

If the stock advances to a point where the profit will pay the cost of the call, you can sell the stock and have the call for nothing.

11. *Average Down*

Assume that the stock you bought has declined in price. You may buy a listed call option on the same stock as a means of averaging down.

If the stock recovers during the time period, either partially or completely, you could end up either with a gain or with your loss reduced.

12. To Shape Tax Destiny

You can use calls to shape, to some extent, your tax destiny.

You could plan in such a way as to make gains on options long-term but losses on options short-term. Hold profitable options over six months to gain long-term profit. Claim short-term losses when you sell unprofitable options just short of six months.

CHAPTER VI

WRITING CALL OPTIONS

Two Normally Irreconcilable Objectives

The writer or seller of call options has two basic objectives: (1) to generate additional income from his stock, and (2) to acquire price protection by at least partially offsetting loss in a falling market.

By its unique features, listed call option writing serves the dual purposes of protecting capital and earning a high income from that capital. These two goals are more often than not irreconcilable with most other investing techniques.

Option writing probably is the only investing approach that starts with cash receipt. The receipt, however, eventually may or may not be a gain. It may just be a downside cushion or may simply lure you into buying stock you wouldn't ordinarily buy. Option writers are paid premium dollars in advance in return for issuing an option contract. This is different from almost all other forms of investing in securities, which call for starting with a cash layout.

Many experienced option writers believe that call buyers are generally wrong in their expectations for moves in the underlying security. They also believe that call buyers who pay relatively high premiums for very short-time periods (usually periods of three to six months) are wrong more often than not.

This belief is, of course, by no means unchallenged. According to some statistics, most options were exercised with gains for the buyers. Many options are believed to have been exercised well in advance of their expiration date.

Active Instead of Passive Role

Listed options have another unique feature in that they assume an active role in contrast to an entirely passive role for an over-the-counter call writer.

In the over-the-counter market a call writer can do nothing but wait for the buyer to call away his stock. More often than not the call buyer may have no wish to do so, since often it would be less expensive for the buyer to convert than to call the stock.

With a liquid options market, the writer can assume an active role. For example, in a sharp rise of the underlying stock, the option loses premium and approaches its intrinsic worth. The writer may repurchase the option, and either sell the next higher strike at a large premium or the call further out at a large premium.

Three Basic Courses

As a writer or seller of a call option, you contract to deliver, upon demand, a specified number of shares at a fixed price, on or before a specified date, to the option buyer. In return the buyer pays you a premium at the time of the option sale.

During the life of the call option, one of the following three basic courses may develop:

(1) The stock moves above the striking price and is called away.

(2) The stock does not move either way and the call expires.

(3) The stock moves below the striking price and the call expires.

Should XYZ rise above the striking price of, say, $50, the buyer would exercise his option and you would be obligated to deliver the stock to him at $50. The loss of the gain you would sustain as a result of the stock's rising above the striking price would be reduced by the premium you have already received.

Should XYZ fail to move either way, or trade below during the life span of the option, you would pocket the premium and retain the stock.

Built-In Advantages

The built-in advantages enjoyed by covered option writers versus long common stock holders or call buyers are obvious, especially in periods of market uncertainties.

In an up market, the covered writer earns the premium and possibly favorable strike price differential. In a flat market, the writer earns the premium. In a down market, the writer may profit if the decline is less than the premium received. The writer loses only when the decline is more than the premium received.

The above advantages are even more compelling when the market is vulnerable to serious correction after a strong and sharp upward movement of the market.

In large part, most of the advantages for option writers are based on the nature of the options instrument itself. It is on the writer's side that the smaller but more consistent dollar is to be made. Accumulation of smaller gains could substantially enhance overall investment returns.

Capital-Protection Features

In addition to augmenting overall portfolio returns, judiciously used listed options can achieve two other important capital-protection objectives, even for conservative portfolios. These are:

1. Reducing net cash outlay in stock purchases through writing call options simultaneously on stocks being bought.
2. Hedging the investment position.

As the national options exchanges expand their coverage of the most widely held and traded stocks, portfolio managers will have more opportunities for option writing.

Besides generating more income, portfolio option writers can, at the same time, limit their downside risk by selling options on core portfolio stocks they would have held through any market decline.

Also, by using stocks in their own portfolio in option writing, portfolio option writers can produce additional income without "churning" their holdings.

Two Sides to a Coin

Every coin has two sides. While the option writer gains downside protection, he may well forgo some of the upside potential.

Should the underlying stock rise substantially, his profit potential is limited to the additional dollars received for selling the option. By writing an option on his underlying security, the security owner gives up an opportunity for any gain resulting from an increase in the price of the underlying stock above the exercise price. In the options market, money made by purchasers represents gains given up on the underlying stocks by the option writers.

Call writers would do well to remember that most of the options they have written have been exercised.

Hedged Percentage

Generally the option writer has to think like a banker, especially in understanding the time value of money. He should look at the market from a mathematical or percentage point of view.

The investment objective of the professional option writer is to achieve a higher-than-normal rate of return on his investment with reduced risk. He favors a hedged percentage by usually forgoing the potential for a large gain. This hedged percentage can be quite considerable on a cumulative basis.

A return of 15 percent to 18 percent a year is possible even for the most conservative writers.

Arithmetic and Reality

For aggressive option writers, options could result in impressive gains on an annualized basis.

For instance, if any option is sold for a 10-percent premium and is exercised in a month, it would amount to an annualized rate of 120 percent, quite astonishing but frequently overlooked arithmetic.

The above annualized rate of return refers only to the

income received by the option writer from the premium, and ignores any price movement of the "long" underlying stock position.

The annualized rate is obtained by dividing the option premium by the current price of the underlying security and adjusting for the length of time remaining in the option.

It should be noted, however, that the exercise of a listed call after one month of its life is very rare. Even in cases that theoretically would justify such an exercise, the call holder can do better by liquidating his call than by exercising it. Only in those cases where the stock has risen so sharply that the option sells for a discount from true worth is there likely to be an early exercise.

"Total Return" Concept

Option-oriented portfolios focus on the "total return" on invested capital from dividends, premiums, and capital gains earned from option writing activities. Unlike options traded over the counter, the writer of listed options retains cash dividends earned on the underlying stock during the time prior to exercise.

The rate of "total return" on an options portfolio could measurably exceed that on a straight debt, equity, or mixed portfolio.

The concept of "total return" on a portfolio has emerged during the past decade, which has witnessed sharp stock market swings.

Cumulative Average Yield

Most high-quality stock portfolios have a cumulative average yield well below that obtainable from high-quality bond portfolios. Now options provide a valid method to increase the yield of high-quality stock portfolios without substantially increasing the risk.

Percentage-minded investors or portfolio managers could do very well by repeatedly selling call options against a portfolio. If judiciously used, option writing can turn a high-quality portfolio into an income portfolio without buying or selling a single stock.

To an increasing number of sophisticated money managers, writing call options is becoming a useful tool to enhance the total portfolio return.

Long-Range Performance

Studies have been made of option writing as a means of improving long-term investment performance.

According to Vincent J. Palermo, manager of the options department at the brokerage firm of Carl Marks & Co., option writing has proved its workability as such a means over a complete market cycle. Mr. Palermo's studies, which covered the past ten years, indicate that writing options on stocks held in a portfolio would produce better investment results than just buying and holding stocks.

Conservative Strategy

In supporting the above conclusion, Mr. Palermo made comparative studies of two institutional-favorite stocks on the basis of option writing versus straight stock purchase and holding. One was IBM, a premier growth stock; the other was General Motors, a leading cyclical stock. Both comparisons led him to believe that writing options is not only actually a conservative strategy but also immeasurably the more lucrative one.

In his comparison studies, Mr. Palermo used certain assumptions, including the existence of a CBOE equivalent, the writing of six-month options in each case, and reasonable option premiums among many other things.

CHAPTER VII

COVERED OPTION WRITING STRATEGIES

Covered and Uncovered

Broadly classified, there are two kinds of options written, covered and uncovered.

A covered option means the writer owns the stock against which he has written an option.

When you sell a covered call the maximum profit is the amount of premium less commission regardless of how much the price of the underlying security may rise.

If an option is written against cash, it is known as an uncovered option—also called a naked option.

An uncovered writer must deposit and maintain sufficient funds with his broker to assure delivery of the stock if the call is exercised. Uncovered option writers expose themselves to great risks. When an investor sells an uncovered call option, the potential for loss is theoretically unlimited.

As long as the naked option is not exercised, it is possible for its writer to realize profits. This has been the case during periods of declining and generally stable stock prices.

Scope of Covered Option

In addition to writing covered options against underlying common stocks, covered options can also be written against warrants, convertible bonds, convertible preferreds, or listed options of the same security. One may even borrow stock to deliver "short." The action that an option writer may choose to take will depend upon his overall strategy as well as his current market judgment.

In the majority of call writings, however, a covered option writer either owns the underlying security or buys it at the time he writes the option.

Generally the writer

(1) Feels comfortable in holding or buying the stock at its present level; and

(2) is willing to sell the stock at the striking price, plus the premium received.

Larger Hedged Component

Since the equity investment is a much larger component of a written position than the option, security selection is the key to a successful writing position.

Fundamentally, option writers would do well to limit writing call options to stocks that are well within their historical price range and P/E relationships. Regular investment criteria should be applied in the stock-selection process.

Determination of Option Value

Some options advisory services have developed proprietary computer programs that regularly evaluate all call option writing opportunities in terms of potential return on investment, downside protection, etc.

While most experts agree on the wisdom of writing an overvalued option and purchasing an undervalued option, the problem of how to determine "overvalued" or "undervalued" options is a real one. Thus the increasing number of options-evaluation services that resort to computer programs to "determine" the "normal value" of an option. When a significant deviation from the "normal value" occurs in the price of an option, it is said to call for purchase or sale of that option accordingly.

"Normal Value" Calculations

The following factors are generally considered the basic components that go into determination of the "normal value": the price and volatility of the stock, the yield of the stock, striking price of the option, and the time remaining before expiration.

(1) *Stock Price*

Since an option sells for a fraction of the price of its underlying security, option value is partly reflective of the value of the underlying security. Everything else being equal, a higher-priced stock normally commands a higher-priced option than a lower-priced stock.

(2) *Stock Volatility*

Option buyers normally are willing to pay more for options underlined by stocks of higher volatility, with correspondingly higher possibilities for profitable exercise or disposal of options.

(3) *Stock Yield*

The impact of stock yield on option value is obvious, because stock yield is part of the total yield on the weighing scale of option writers. Higher stock yield may compensate for lower option premium return. By the same token, the level of money cost also is reflected in option price. Higher money cost to maintain the option writer's stock position causes him to compensate for it with a higher option premium.

(4) *Option Striking Price*

The direct relationship between the striking price and option value is apparent.

(5) *Time Factor*

Since options are wasting assets and vanish in value at expiration, time is an important factor in the determination of their value. Everything else being equal, longer-duration options normally command a higher price than shorter-duration options. As a general rule, the diminishing rate in the value of an option accelerates toward the end of the time period. "In the money" options, however, maintain their value almost to the last day of expiration.

Combined with fundamental research on underlying securities, "normal value" calculations help determine the most advantageous striking price and expiration date of the options to be written or bought.

More Used by Writers than Buyers

While "normal value" calculations are also very useful to option buyers in search for value, such calculations are more frequently used by option writers than by option buyers.

This is because, for one thing, option writers depend more on such calculations to locate call-writing situations that are believed to be overvalued. For another, the "normal value" concept helps option writers to know how to close out their positions—usually just when the option reaches "normal value."

Broad Option Writing Strategies

Based on the "total return" concept discussed in Chapter VI, option writing can be designed to cope with varying market conditions.

In a stable and moderately advancing market, option writers seek a rate of return that is higher than that obtainable by nonwriters.

In a declining market, option writing portfolio risks are cushioned by premiums received.

Generally it would be more desirable for writers to issue calls for the more distant contract months. For one thing, they yield more premium dollars, which also serve to provide more protection against downside risk. For another, they would make it possible to earn long-term capital gains from option premiums. To be avoided is writing call options that are shorter than six months and that generate less than $200 in option premium.

The following are several of the most important call option writing strategies:

1. *Intermediate-Term Hedge*

When option writers believe certain stocks are due for an intermediate-term consolidation after a sharp rise, they may take in premium money while waiting for further gains.

2. *To Sell at Above-Market Price*

Option writing is used as a means of selling stocks already owned at a price level above the current market. Even if the price of the stock were to decline, the option writer is better off—by the amount of the premium—than if he had not written an option.

3. *"Buy-Back"*

If the underlying security declines to a level that forfeits most of the option premium received, consideration should be given to disposing of the stock.

If the writer decides to sell the stock, he should "buy back" the outstanding call obligation to eliminate the remaining time exposure.

4. *Buy-Stop Order*

As an added defense to the above strategy, option writers should try to limit the risk that might result from a sharp price recovery by entering a buy-stop order to purchase a second 100-share position in XYZ at the original strike price. At the expiration of both calls, option writers might sell still a third call option to take in additional premium.

5. *Step-Down Protection*

As a variation of the above strategy, option writers might retain the stock, despite the price drop, in the following way: buy back the outstanding call obligation to eliminate the remaining time exposure, thus paving the way for selling more-distant calls that invariably carry larger premiums.

This strategy is based upon the assumption that the second more-distant call is written at the same striking price as the first. Should a call with a lower striking price become available, the writer could issue such a call with new premium to shelter him from a further stock-price drop.

6. *Means of Creating Short-Term Loss*

Options can be written as a means of creating short-term losses.

Assume you sold a call option on 100 shares of XYZ
that you bought at $50. Assume that after a period
of six months and one day XYZ has advanced to
$100.

At this point you decide to sell XYZ at 100, which results in a long-term capital gain of $5,000. At the
same time you buy another 100 shares of XYZ at
100. With XYZ at 100, your original call option
with the striking price of $50 would be exercised
against you and you fulfill your obligation by deliv-
ering the second 100 shares of XYZ purchased at
100, resulting in a short-term loss of $5,000, less the
premium.

In effect you will have transferred approximately
$5,000 (less option premium) from the short-term
gain column to the long-term column, assuming
that you have already amassed that much short-
term gain.

CHAPTER VIII

ELEMENTS OF OPTION WRITING PORTFOLIOS

Measures of Option Premium

Since the call writer's potential profits are limited to option premiums, methods of measuring premium are of paramount importance.

The size of the premium can be assessed from the viewpoint of return as well as from that of risk protection.

Return and Protection

From the viewpoint of return, premium plus dividends should be large enough to earn an annual return of approximately 20 percent, if not more. From the viewpoint of risk protection, downside protection in the form of premium should be no less than 10 percent of the writer's commitment.

Option writing for return and protection is based on the following criteria:

    1. Return on Cash Flow (R. C. F.), which is the immediate return on actual dollar commitment, indicating leverage based on cash flow.

$$R.\ C.\ F.^* = \frac{\text{call option premium (OP)}}{\text{market price of stock (MP)}}$$

2. Maximum Yield on Investment (M. Y.), which represents the theoretically maximum realizable return under optimal conditions.

$$M.\ Y.\ = \frac{OP + (SP - MP) + D}{MP}$$

OP = Call Premium
SP = Striking Price
MP = Market Price
D = Expected Dividend (until option expiration)

3. Annualized Return (A. R.), which represents a conservative estimate of annual return based on the maximum length of holding period.

$$A.\ R. = \frac{360}{\text{number of days to expiration}} \times \text{the lesser of}$$
$$\text{R.C.F. or M.Y.}$$

4. Downside Breakeven (D. B.), which constitutes the downside price for breakeven.
D. B. = MP − OP − D

*For simplification, R. C. F. is calculated on the basis of cash stock purchase, instead of on margin. For margin account, its leverage is increased by a multiplier of two, as follows:

$$R.\ C.\ F. = \frac{OP}{MP}\ (2)$$

5. Downside Breakeven Percentage (D. B. P.), which represents the percentage of stock decline for breakeven

$$\frac{MP-D.B.}{MP}$$

Trade-Off

Option writing selection essentially is a trade-off between downside protection and expected return.

Normally, such return declines as downside protection increases.

Maximum Return

In one-to-one option writing the maximum return to the writer, before dividends, is the difference, on the one hand, between the striking price plus the option price and the stock price on the other, assuming that the market price is lower than the striking price. The maximum return occurs at expiration when the stock sells at or above the option's exercise price and is not exercised.

The principal source of the option writer's gain will come from option premium. He will benefit, however, also from any increase in the stock price up to the exercise price.

Premium with or without Tangible Worth

There is difference between premium with or without tangible worth.

For a call option with tangible worth or intrinsic value, the premium represents the excess differential between the current stock price and the option's exercise price. For a call option without intrinsic value, the entire option price represents its premium.

94

Low-P/E-and-High-Yield Writing Portfolios

For conservative option writers, the core of their writing portfolios should be stocks with low P/E and high yields. The following is illustrative of such portfolios, based on February 24, 1975, closing prices:

	1974-75 high-low	2/24 stock price	P/E	Div'd	Yield	2/24 option price
Penn-zoil	30½ -12¾	20¼	6	$1.20	5.9%	2½ (July 20)
Gen. Tel.	26⅝ -16⅛	21¾	10	$1.80	8.3%	2⅛ (Apr. 20)
Texaco	32⅞ -20	26¼	4	$2.00	7.6%	2¾ (July 25)
Gulf	25¼ -16	20⅝	4	$1.70	8.3%	3 (Oct. 20)
Good-year	18⅜ -11¾	15¾	7	$1.10	7.0%	2⅜ (July 15)
Kenne-cott	49½ -25⅜	33¼	6	$2.60	7.8%	2¾ (July 35)
U. S. Steel	50 -35⅜	49¼	4	$2.80	5.7%	4⅛ (July 50)

Possible Workout Against Key Measurements

The following is a summary of possible workout on above recommendations against key measurements.

	Return on Cash Flow (R. C. F.)	Maximum Yield on Investment (M. Y.)	Annualized Return (A. R.)	Downside Breakeven (D. B.)	Percentage of Decline for Breakeven (D. B. P.)
Pennzoil	12.3%	12.3%	29.5%	$17.25	14.8%
Gen. Tel	13.8%	9.2%	22.1%	$18.00	17.2%
Texaco	10.5%	9.0%	21.6%	$22.67	13.6%
Gulf	10.3%	11.3%	24.7%	$16.92	18.0%
Goodyear	15.0%	13.2%	31.7%	$12.92	18.0%
Kennecott	8.3%	16.8%	19.9%	$29.42	11.5%
U.S. Steel	8.4%	12.3%	20.2%	$43.96	10.8%

PENNZOIL

Stock price = 20¼ (2/24)   P/E = 6
Dividends = $1.20   Yield = 5.9%

Option Strategy
>   Buy stock at 20¼ (2/24)
>   Sell July 20 call option at 2½

Option Worksheet
>   (1) Return on Cash Flow = 12.3%
>   (2) Maximum Yield on Investment = 12.3%
>   (3) Annualized Return = 29.5%
>   (4) Downside Breakeven = $17.25
>   (5) Downside Breakeven Percentage = 14.8%

GENERAL TELEPHONE & ELECTRONICS

Stock Price=21¾ (2/24)
Dividends=$1.80

P/E=10
Yield=8.3%

Option Strategy
> Buy stock at 21¾ (2/24)
> Sell July 20 option at 3 (2/24)

Option Worksheet
> (1) Return on Cash Flow=13.8%
> (2) Maximum Yield on Investment=9.2%
> (3) Annualized Return=22.1%
> (4) Downside Breakeven=$18.00
> (5) Downside Breakeven Percentage=17.2%

TEXACO

Stock price=26¼ (2/24)
Dividends=$2

P/E=4
Yield=7.6%

Option Strategy
> Buy stock at 26¼ (2/24)
> Sell July 25 call option at 2¾ (2/24)

Option Worksheet
> (1) Return on Cash Flow=10.5%
> (2) Maximum Yield on Investment=9.0%
> (3) Annualized Return=21.6%
> (4) Downside Breakeven=$22.67
> (5) Downside Breakeven Percentage=13.6%

GULF OIL

Stock price=20⅝ (2/24)   P/E=4
Dividends=$1.70   Yield=8.3%

Option Strategy
  Buy stock at 20⅝ (2/24)
  Sell July 20 option at 3 (2/24)

Option Worksheet
  (1) Return on Cash Flow=10.3%
  (2) Maximum Yield on Investment=11.3%
  (3) Annualized Return=24.7%
  (4) Downside Breakeven=$16.92
  (5) Downside Breakeven Percentage=18.0%

GOODYEAR TIRE & RUBBER

Stock price=15¾   P/E=7
Dividends=$1.10   Yield=7.0%

Option Strategy
  Buy stock at 15¾ (2/24)
  Sell July 15 option at 2⅜ (2/24)

Option Worksheet
  (1) Return on Cash Flow=15.0%
  (2) Maximum Yield on Investment=13.2%
  (3) Annualized Return=31.7%
  (4) Downside Breakeven=$12.92
  (5) Downside Breakeven Percentage=18.0%

KENNECOTT

Stock price=33¼   P/E=6
Dividends=$2.60   Yield=7.8%

Option Strategy
Buy stock at 33¼ (2/24)
Sell July 35 option at 2¾ (2/24)

Option Worksheet
(1) Return on Cash Flow=8.3%
(2) Maximum Yield on Investment=16.8%
(3) Annualized Return=19.9%
(4) Downside Breakeven=$29.42
(5) Downside Breakeven Percentage=11.5%

U.S. STEEL

Stock price=49¼   P/E=4
Dividends=$2.80   Yield=5.7%

Option Strategy
Buy stock at 49¼ (2/24)
Sell July 50 option at 4⅛ (2/24)

Option Worksheet
(1) Return on Cash Flow=8.4%
(2) Maximum Yield on Investment=12.3%
(3) Annualized Return=20.2%
(4) Downside Breakeven=$43.96
(5) Downside Breakeven Percentage=10.8%

Portfolio Strategy
Buy 1,000 shares of each of the above seven stocks.
Sell 10 calls on each above stock.

Portfolio Investment and Projected Returns

Based on Annualized Returns projected earlier, the following is a summary of portfolio investment and its possible returns (see Option Worksheets above).

	1,000-sh. purchase	Cost of cash purchase	Annualized Return	
			Percentage	Dollars
Pennzoil	10×$2,025	$20,250	29.5%	$5,974
Texaco	10×$2,625	$26,250	21.6%	$5,670
Gen. Tel	10×$2,175	$21,750	22.1%	$4,807
Gulf	10×$2,063	$20,630	24.7%	$5,096
Goodyear	10×$1,575	$15,750	31.7%	$4,993
Kennecott	10×$3,325	$33,250	19.9%	$6,617
U.S. Steel	10×$4,925	$49,250	20.2%	$9,949
		$187,130		$43,106

The above projected $43,106 annualized return on $187,130 investment (based on 100-percent cash purchase) would amount to a portfolio return of 23.0 percent.

The percentage return would be much greater if a 50-percent margin instead of 100-percent cash is used.

Portfolio Balance

Most of the striking prices used in the above examples are close to the present marked prices of their underlying securities.

Generally, conservative equity portfolios write longer-term options at strike prices lower than the current market price of the underlying security.

On the other hand, the more aggressive equity portfolios incline toward shorter-term options with strike prices that are above the current market price of the security.

A proper balance between longer-term-strike-below-market writes and shorter-term-strike-above-market writes should be structured, varying with individual portfolios, depending upon their relative emphasis on return and capital protection.

Options-Oriented Portfolios

A properly structured options-oriented portfolio is designed to produce returns of 20 percent to 25 percent, indicating gains of from $20,000 to $25,000 on an option capital of $100,000 that is believed to be required for writing call options on a diversified list of stocks. This 20-percent to 25-percent gain will provide a downside cushion of like amounts in a down market. In other words, the option writer could still break even despite a 20-percent to 25-percent decline in his portfolio.

To achieve appreciation objectives of 20 percent to 25 percent, it stands to reason that options-oriented portfolios should exclude writing any call options of premium sizes that, if exercised on expiration date, would produce less than a 20-percent annualized return. Nor would such portfolios consider writing options with premiums that provide less than 10 percent downside protection.

IF-CALLED-AWAY-OPTION WRITING PORTFOLIOS

Major Reservoir

One major reservoir of call writing situations that helps achieve the dual objectives of return and protection for options-oriented portfolios is the writing of call options with an eye toward their called-away possibilities.

Two covered writing categories offer the potential for attractive returns should the underlying stocks be called away or remain unchanged.

Short-Term-If-Called-Away Writes

The following situations are designed to illustrate if-called-away call options for possible realization of gains over the short term:

Illustration #1

On May 5, 1975, the writing of either the July 40 option (premium 2⅝) or the October 40 option (premium 4⅛) against Kennecott common (NYSE-38-KN) offered the potential for attractive returns should the underlying stock be called away.

The KN July 40 option would bring in 2⅝ points in option premium which, plus two points from appreciation of the stock should it be called away at 40, would total 4⅝ points or 13.1 percent on an 11-week option or 61.9 percent annualized, exclusive of dividends.

The KN October 40 option would produce 4⅛ points which, together with the same two-point appreciation, would total 6⅛ or 18.1 percent over the short term or 85.6 percent annualized.

Special Situation Value

A possible special situation was developing at KN as its value was bulwarked by the pending divestiture of the Peabody Coal subsidiary. A 6.8-percent yield was available on dividends of $2.60. Its P/E ratio of 10.4 was indicated on estimated 1975 earnings of $3.65.

Since a severe recession undoubtedly cuts current earnings ability of most basic industries, investment stress should be laid on U.S.-based resources companies, particularly those with favorable supply-demand relationships once recession recedes.

Technically, KN was emerging strongly from a several-month sidewise move, as indicated by attainment of

102

recovery highs on expanded volume.

Illustration #2

Another if-called-away call writing possibility existed on
May 5, 1975, when the sale of the July 45 call option at 4¾
against 100 shares of Deere (NYSE-45½-DE) would protect
the stock down to 40¾.

If DE were called away at 45, the gains for the option
writer would amount to 4¼ plus dividends, less commissions.

Recession-Resistant

Fundamentally DE was favorably situated as the
technological leader in agricultural equipment, a vitally important American industry that should continue to prosper
despite recession as a growing world population depends on
U.S. farmers for sustenance. Estimated 1975 earnings of
$6.20 indicated a P/E ratio of 7.3 versus its 12-year average
P/E of 10.5. A 4-percent yield on indicated dividends of
$1.80.

Technically, DE remained bullish after a sharp move
from the September low of 28. While a long-term objective
of beyond 60 was projected from the underlying base formation, interim profits appeared possible for a number of
writing operations.

Illustration #3

Also illustrative of short-term hedges was possible writing on May 5, 1975, of a July 30 call option on American
Cyanamid (NYSE-28¾-ACY) to produce 2¼ points in option premium that would protect the stock down to 26½.

For 11 weeks available on this short-term option, a return of 8.5 percent or 40.2 percent annualized was indicated, exclusive of dividends. Should the stock be called

away at expiration, the writer would realize an additional appreciation of 1¼ points which, plus 2¼ points from option premium, would total 3½ points or 13.2 percent on 11 weeks or 62.4 percent annualized.

Fundamentally, a streamlined ACY was expected to hold its ground in a recession year. Technically, ACY had an overall favorable pattern.

Intermediate-Term-If-Called-Away Writes

Six-month call options are generally used in writing intermediate-term options for possible if-called-away situations.

Illustration #4

On June 3, 1975, such an intermediate-term writing situation existed in the sale of an October 15 call option at 3¼ against 100 shares of Merrill Lynch (NYSE-16¼-MER), thereby reducing the cash outlay to 13 on a fully paid cash basis.

If MER remains unchanged at expiration, the covered writer would realize $385, including $325 from option premium and $60 from dividends, or 29.6% return in 19 weeks.

Technically MER has paused in the 14–18 zone within an overall favorable formation.

Illustration #5

Another illustration of this type of call writing was Federal National Mortgage which, on April 21, 1975, was available for 17.

Its October 20 option produced 1¾ points in option premium, plus 3 points from appreciation on stock if called away at 20, that would realize a total of 4¾ points, indicating a return of 70% in six months, or 140% annualized, on cash investment of $675 for a margin account (50% margin on stock, less $175 in option premium).

Illustration #6

Another if-called-away writing possibility was available on June 3, 1975, that would involve the purchase of 100 shares of Ford (NYSE-36⅝-F) and the sale of an October 40 option at 4.

Should the F October 40 call be exercised, the return to the writer would amount to $8.58, including four points from option premium, $1.20 from dividends, and 3⅜ from appreciation, indicating a return of 26.3%.

Technically, Ford continued in a long-term base area.

Buy-Wait-Write

Writers of call options with an eye toward their called-away possibilities can either buy shares and concurrently write calls against them or buy shares first and then wait for some appreciation before writing calls against them.

Illustrative of such a course was the possible purchase on April 21, 1975, of Delta (NYSE-36-DAL).

An option premium of 4½ was available to a DAL October 40 option writer. This premium, plus 3¾ points from appreciation on the stock if called away, would realize 8¼ points, indicating a return of 42.9 percent in six months or 85.7 percent annualized on cash investment of $1,350 for margin account (50% margin on stock, less $450 in option premium).

Another possible working-through of a strategy involving buying of stock first and waiting for higher option premium was evident to those who bought Tesoro Petroleum (NYSE-TSO) first at 16 on April 21, 1975, and then waited until it reached the 20 level before writing options to gain higher option premium.

By May 20, 1975, TSO reached 19⅝. The option writer was now in a position to sell the July 15 option at 5, thereby protecting the stock down to 14⅝ or 25 percent.

No More Speculative

The selling of options against a portfolio is no more speculative than is the owning of stocks themselves.

Options are sold by individuals, funds, trusts, or anyone who has "a continuous portfolio of common stocks."

Previously, while long-term growth segments of portfolios were used to take care of future actuarial funding obligations and as a hedge against inflation, separate segments of portfolios were geared toward income in order to meet current obligations.

As options on more of the most widely held common stocks begin to be traded on the national options exchanges, fund fiduciaries will expand their option writing operations to take advantage of the high total yields obtainable.

For at least the next few years, buyers will likely continue to outnumber writers, giving the writer an extra advantage. However, in perhaps five years, if not much sooner, trust departments will be writing options as a matter of normal business.

CHAPTER IX

VARIABLE HEDGING STRATEGIES

Completely and Partially Uncovered

Since variable hedging primarily deals with partially uncovered option writing, it serves as a bridge between covered and uncovered option writing. A full understanding of uncovered option writing should precede our discussions of variable hedging or ratio option writing strategies.

UNCOVERED OPTION WRITING

Naked Writers

An uncovered or "naked" option is written without the writer owning the underlying stock.

Essentially, naked option writing is based on the belief that, generally, call option buyers as a group are wrong within their time frame.

Principally market bears, naked option writers speculate on a downward course of the stock during the life of their contracts.

So long as the option is not exercised, it is possible for writers of uncovered options to realize profits. This has been the case during periods of declining or generally stable stock prices.

Writing Against Cash

An uncovered or naked option is written against cash. It represents substantial risk, should there be a sharp rise in the price of the underlying stock.

As an example, our option writer might decide that XYZ is not a stock he wishes to own. But, since he considers the premium to be attractive, he decides to sell the call without owning the stock.

He must post the required minimum 30-percent margin, reduced by the amount of premium. In a sense he is now in a short position.

If XYZ declines, the entire option premium will be profit, although only ordinary income.

But if XYZ rises, he may at some future date be forced to choose between buying the stock in the open market to cover the call or assuming an actual short position at the striking price with the stock selling at a higher price level, or buying back the option for an ordinary loss.

Extremely Risky

Uncovered option writing is extremely risky and a naked writer may incur large losses, limited only by the amount of the increase in the price of the underlying security.

Only very sophisticated investors of substantial means should engage in uncovered writing. The exchanges require substantial cash from sellers of naked options to assure themselves that the option writers (or sellers) will be able to meet their obligations.

In addition to maintaining a specified amount of margin on deposit in his account, an uncovered option writer may at any time be called upon to purchase the underlying security at its then-prevailing market price in order to be able to deliver it at the striking (exercise) price.

Moreover, the uncovered (naked) writer has no control over when he might be required to buy and deliver the underlying security. Indeed, he may be given an exercise

108

notice at any time when the underlying security price exceeds the exercise price.

Assuming an extremely high degree of risk, uncovered option writers seek much larger gains percentagewise than those that are sought by the more conservative covered option writers. The maximum profits for uncovered writers, however, are limited by the premium paid for the option by the buyers, less commissions. On the other hand, the risk to uncovered writers is unlimited until they close their positions. To reduce their risk exposure, naked option writers tend to write short-term call options.

Not Unlike "Short" Sale

In assessing risk, uncovered option writing is not unlike a "short" sale of the underlying stock. Each transaction generally has the same effective exposure, except that the uncovered option writer's risk is cushioned somewhat by the amount of the premium.

Possible Recourses

What could happen when an option writer selling a naked call is wrong about the stock and finds himself in a bind when the stock on which he has sold a naked call option rises in price?

What are the possible courses of action to defend his position, if the market begins to move away from a naked seller?

Defense #1—"Buy In"

Like the covered writer, an uncovered writer may usually cancel his obligation at any time prior to being assigned an exercise notice by executing a "closing purchase" transaction, thus terminating his obligation to deliver the stock.

In other words, the naked option writer can "buy in"

an option he has previously written, providing the option hasn't already been exercised. His gain or loss depends on the difference between the premium originally received and the price later paid.

Defense #2—Taking Cover

An uncovered option writer may also, during the life of the option, buy the underlying security, thereby becoming a covered writer.

This "taking cover" would amount to a substantial investment in a stock about which he was wrong.

Defense #3—Offsetting Call Option

The uncovered option writer may buy an offsetting call option on the same security to cover his "naked" option sale.

As an example, if he sold the McDonald option naked at 50 and got worried when the underlying shares reached 60, he would simply buy a call on McDonald at 60.

Defense #4—"Buy-Stop"

A fourth course of defense is to enter a "buy-stop" order at a price that is generally calculated on the basis of the striking price plus option premium. The purpose of the "buy-stop" order is to limit an unknown loss.

PARTIALLY UNCOVERED OPTION WRITING

Hedged Strategies

Instead of completely naked writing, the writer may choose to hedge his position partially. He may wish to combine the writing of covered and uncovered options on the same underlying stock.

Known as variable hedging or ratio writing, this strategy involves writing one option that is covered and one or more options that are uncovered.

The additional downside protection provided by the additional premium income, however, must be weighed against the risk of incurring a loss on the option—or options—that are uncovered.

Writing Multiple Options

Since the premium is a small percentage of the price of the underlying stock, a significant decline in the price of the stock can quickly wipe out the protection offered by the premium.

An alternative course: write more than one call to achieve greater price protection. The sale of two options will allow the price of the underlying stock to decline further before your hedge position will show a loss, because you will have twice the premium to offset a decline in the price of the underlying stock. Also, you will benefit from lower commissions per option.

When the underlying security sells at a price far below the strike price, aggressive writers tend to increase the number of calls per 100 shares of stock. They may own 100 shares and issue two or more calls.

Variety of Hedges

An investor who is moderately bearish might wish to sell three calls against a 200-share "long" position.

A more aggressive writer, convinced of a more substantial downside move, might sell two or even three calls against a 100-share "long" position.

These combinations provide a variety of hedges and are attractive to a writer seeking greater protection when he anticipates a declining market in the underlying stock.

How To Determine "Ratio"

When a ratio writer determines the number of calls to be written against a 100-share position, the ratio is a function of his risk preference.

In the determination of the ratio to be written, the upside risk from uncovered options should be weighed against the additional downside protection.

"Position One, Sell Two" Strategy

The most frequently employed ratio writing is to "position one, sell two," i.e., buy 100 shares of stock and issue two call options.

The general belief motivating option writers for the "position one, sell two" strategy is that most stocks generally fluctuate, in a six-month period, within a range of no more than 25 percent above and 25 percent below the striking price.

A profit-protection zone generally sought by ratio writers applying the "position one, sell two" strategy extends 25 percent up and 25 percent down from the striking price. The closer to the striking price the underlying security remains, the greater the profit to the writer becomes.

Selection Criteria

Thus, in selecting stocks for "position one, sell two" writing, hedge writers generally favor those that are likely to stay within the parameters of their protection zone and, preferably, close to the striking price.

"Profit Band"

The protection zone covered by these two parameters constitutes the "profit band." Ratio writers will remain profitable so long as the stock stays between the upside and downside parameters.

These upside and downside parameters also constitute the upside and downside breakeven points.

Downside Parameter
Downside parameter is obtained by reducing the purchase price by the total premium received from writing two or more call options.

Upside Parameter
Upside parameter is computed by more complicated formulas, as follows:

(1) When stock cost is below the striking price:

$$\frac{\text{premium received added to the difference between stock cost and strike price}}{\text{number of uncovered options}} \quad \text{plus strike price}$$

(2) When stock cost is above the striking price:

$$\frac{\text{premium received less the difference between strike price and stock cost}}{\text{number of uncovered options}} \quad \text{plus strike price}$$

How To Establish "Profit Band"
The following are several illustrations of how to establish a "profit band" for ratio writers.

Illustration #1
On June 3, 1975, a ratio writer may have wished to sell two October 45 calls at 5½ per call on a 100-share "long" position on Syntex (NYSE-43⅝-SYN).

The 11 points from option premium protect the stock

down to 32⅝ as the downside parameter. The upside parameter is 57³/₈.

A profit band of from 32⅝ to 57⅜, amounting to 24¾ points, is thus established, within which the partial hedger will realize a profit.

Technically SYN had marked time between 38 and 45 after its recent run-up.

Illustration #2

Based on April 21, 1975, closing prices, another illustrative ratio writing, also on Syntex, appeared attractive as follows: writing two Syntex October 40 calls at 8⅝ each against 100 shares at 43⅛.

The sale of two calls realized 17¼ points which protected the 100 share position down to 25⅞ or 40 percent below the current market. The breakeven point was only 2¾ points above Syntex's lowest price during the 1973–75 period.

No upside loss would occur until the 54 area is reached.

Broad Profit Possibility

Thus, a wide profit zone of 28¼ points was created between 54⅛ and 25⅞.

The above strategy provides a broad profit possibility without having to guess correctly which direction the stock or the market will take.

Illustration #3

An aggressive ratio writer on June 3, 1975, might have considered selling two July 80 calls at 4¾ points per call of Xerox (NYSE-76¼-XRX) against 100 shares of stock purchased.

The premiums from the two calls, totaling 9½ points,

114

protected the stock down to 66¾ as the downside parameter. The upside parameter was 93¼.

The above parameters would establish a 26½-point profit range from 66¾ to 93¼. A short-term reaction was indicated for XRX.

Illustration #4

Another ratio writing appeared sensible on Avon Products (NYSE-48⅝-AVP) on June 5, 1975, when the ratio writer could sell two October 50 calls at 6⅛ per call. The option premiums, totaling 12¼ points, would protect the stock down to 36⅜ points. The upside profit limit was 63⅝.

The ratio writer would remain profitable so long as AVP swings within the 27¼-point zone (between 63⅝ and 36⅜)

Illustration #5

Another illustration of this ratio writing method was the possible purchase on June 5, 1975, of 100 shares of Disney (NYSE-51¼-DIS) and the sale of two January 60 calls at 6⅝ per call.

The 13¼ points from option premiums would protect the stock down to 38 as the downside parameter. The upside parameter was 82.

The ratio writer would remain profitable so long as DIS fluctuates in the broad range of 38 to 82.

DIS's primary uptrend started to ease as it came under increasing selling pressures.

Modified Strategy

As a modification of the above strategy, the option writer may decide initially to write only one option for each 100 shares of stock owned—then subsequently to write a second option with a lower exercise price if there is a de-

115

crease in the price of the underlying stock.

Three-Against-One Strategy

To provide additional defense against a possible deep downward move is the three-against-one strategy.

Illustrative of this ratio strategy was the possible sale on April 21, 1975, of three October 50 calls on Homestake Mining (NYSE-43⅞-HM) against 100 shares. At 5 each, the three calls would realize $1,500, protecting the stock position down to 28⅞ or 34 percent below the market.

No upside loss would occur until 60 9/16. Thus a profit zone of 31 11/16 points was created.

The above 3-to-1 strategy on HM was primarily for a venturesome hedger who was not particularly bullish on gold stocks.

CHAPTER X

PUT OPTION STRATEGIES

Proper Perspective

While no listed put options are yet available, this book would fail to give the reader a proper perspective on the option market without some analysis of put options.

Also, an understanding of the basic put option strategies is prerequisite to the chapters following on straddles and other option variations, since such option variations are created by combining the two basic types of options, namely, call options and put options. For instance, a straddle is a contract consisting of one call and one put with identical contractual terms.

A Call in Reverse

A put option is a call option in reverse. A put is an option to sell a specified number of shares of a specific stock at a fixed price, within a designated time period.

In the over-the-counter market, put options constitute a very small percentage of total option purchases. This is due to the simple supply-and-demand factor. The less demand for put options results from the tendency on the part of investment houses toward buying (call) options rather than selling (put) options. The result is, generally, lower premiums for put options than for call options. There are times, however, when put premiums are equal to, or exceed, call premiums.

Two Sides of a Game

Just as call options have two sides to the game, put options also involve buying on the one side and writing (selling) on the other.

On the buying side, a speculator buys a call option when he believes the underlying security will rise in value and buys a put option when he thinks the underlying security will decline in value.

On the writing (selling) side, a speculator sells a put option when he believes the underlying security will go up and sells a call option when he thinks the underlying security will fall.

Anticipating a Declining Market

It is possible to make money in a falling market as well as in a rising one.

Put option purchases and short sales are the two principal means of profiting from a declining stock if the put option buyer or the short seller is correct in his judgment.

For instance, if, on June 10, 1975, a trader believed Xerox (NYSE-69¾-XRX) would fall substantially, he bought, for $400, a 95-day put option on XRX at 69¾. If XRX declined in price, he would buy back XRX in the open market and utilize his put option to sell it out at 69¾, pocketing the difference between his purchase price and the striking price less expenses. Or he may resell his put with the same net result.

If, instead of declining, XRX went up, the put option would become worthless, with a resulting loss of purchase premium of $400 on the part of the put option buyer.

118

Only Source of Supply

Since it will be some time before listed put options become available on the national options exchanges, the over-the-counter market is the only source of supply for put options.

How To Select Time-Period Value

Generally six-month-ten-day put options constitute the best time-period value for one's money among put options traded over the counter.

For one thing, these longer-term options cost relatively less in premium than shorter-term options. For another, generally there is a large supply of relatively longer-term options from writers.

Finally, from a tax point of view, a profitable put option held longer than six months is entitled to long-term capital gain tax treatment.

Alternate Course

As an alternative to buying a put option in the above Xerox instance, the trader may choose to sell XRX short at 69¾.

If XRX did go down, the trader would realize a profit by buying 100 XRX to close out his short sale. If, on the other hand, XRX went up, he might eventually be forced to cover his short position by buying XRX higher than 69¾ and end up with a loss.

Put Option Versus Short Sale

Since a put option and a short sale are two different means of achieving essentially the same objective, what are their relative merits and demerits?

For one thing, a short sale entails greater risks than taking a long position in that, while a stock can only decline to zero, there is no theoretical limit to how high it might rise. On the other hand, instead of unlimited risks incurred by a short sale, a put option can accomplish the same purpose while limiting risk to the cost of the option.

For another, a put option has distinctly important tax advantages over a short sale.

Improved Means

Comparatively few people sell short in the stock market. One of the principal factors that discourage selling short to seek profits are Internal Revenue Service rules on the taxing of regular short sale profits. Its rules call for all regular short sale profits to be taxed as short-term gains.

Put options provide an improved means of shorting without the penalty of having short sale profits taxed as short-term gains.

Important Tax Advantage

While this book will summarize tax factors affecting options in a later section, it appears appropriate here to stress the important tax advantage that puts have over short sales.

Under Internal Revenue Service rules, no short position can result in a long-term gain. Profits made on a short sale are always short-term for tax purposes, regardless of how long one is "short" the stock.

On the other hand, when 100 shares of stock and a put option on the same stock are bought simultaneously, the short sale rule does not always apply.

An exemption from the short sale rule occurs when the put option is identified as a hedge; that is, the put option is used to sell the stock or allowed to expire. In that case, for tax purposes the holding period begins with the date of acquiring the stock.

The short sale rule applies only if the put option is

separately resold or exercised to sell stock acquired at a different date.

Special Tax Rule

Since the difference in tax treatment of gains from put options and from short sales accounts for the principal advantage of buying put options over short selling, it is appropriate to trace the origin of this difference.

Under an Internal Revenue Service special rule, the acquisition of a put option is considered to be the making of a short sale and the exercise or the expiration of the put option is treated as the closing of a short sale.

Exception to Special Tax Rule

An exception to that special rule occurs when (1) the stock and the put option are acquired on the same date, and (2) the stock is identified as intended to be used in exercising the put option.

If these two requirements are met, the acquisition of the put option will not be treated as a short sale and the special rule will not be applicable.

According to an Internal Revenue Service ruling, the premium received from the sale of a put option is construed as reducing the acquisition price of the underlying security if the put option is exercised. Therefore premiums obtained from exercised put options are eligible for capital gain tax treatment. On the other hand, premiums obtained from unexercised put options are construed as ordinary income.

In contrast, no short position qualifies for capital gain tax treatment under any circumstances.

Long-Term Profit in Falling Market

The only ways to achieve possible long-term profits in a declining market are through purchase of put options good for more than six months and through sale of put options after they have been held over six months, if the decline in the stocks is large enough to show profits.

Instead of Buy-Stop

A put option has another important advantage over a short position protected by a buy-stop.

A put option is more desirable than a stop-loss, which is designed for the primary purpose of protecting a major portion of unrealized profit. On the other hand, a stop order could not benefit from a renewed price rise after a temporary price break that may trigger a stop order.

Since, many times, the New York Stock Exchange bans buy-stop orders, the stop order provides no guarantee of execution at the specified price.

PUT OPTION BUYING TECHNIQUES

Put options are purchased for a significant number of uses and with varying techniques.

Hedges Against Existing Positions

An ever-growing number of options are bought as hedges against existing positions. Just as a call option can guarantee the purchase price of a short position, a put option can guarantee the sale price of a long position.

Protecting a Long Position

A put option can be bought to protect a paper profit that has already accrued.

Assume that a stock that you had purchased at $50 has advanced to $70. If you become concerned about possible erosion of your paper profit in an uncertain market, one means of defense is to buy, say, a 95-day put option at $70 for, perhaps, $350.

Protective Premium

If your concern proves groundless and the stock continues its upward course, you simply allow the put option to expire. Your loss would be limited to $350 as the cost of this protective premium. It amounts to the cost of buying an insurance policy to protect you from the unexpected.

On the other hand, should your concern about possible erosion of your paper profit prove to be well founded and the stock retreats to 50, you could exercise your put option and sell the stock at $70. Instead of having your paper profit of $2,000 completely wiped out, you would keep the bulk of that profit intact, namely, $1,650 out of $2,000.

Insulate Short-Term Breaks

Put options can be purchased as a means of protecting the unrealized profits in stocks you own, especially when you are doubtful about their short-term possibilities but are still very bullish about their long-term prospects.

In the above case, when you are concerned about possible erosion of your paper profit of $2,000 when the stock has risen from $50 to $70, some might advise placing a sell-stop order 5 percent to 10 percent below the market.

This sell-stop order would accomplish the primary purpose of protecting a major portion of the profit. However, while the stock might go down to a price level that would activate a stop order, the stock might then turn around and rise to new highs.

Purchase of a put option provides the best means of avoiding this latter possibility and insulating the stock from short-term breaks.

Trading for Down Fluctuations

Under the protective umbrella of a put option, one can play the down fluctuations of the stock.

This trading technique involves making a number of short-term gains through buying the stock on dips and then selling the stock out on rallies.

There is no limitation to the number of trades that can be made against a particular put option within a given period of time. While the profit potential of such trading can be substantial, its risk is limited by the cost of the put option.

Put options can also be traded against call options. By trading against a call option, a put option functions to assure a riskless stock market transaction.

PUT OPTION WRITING TECHNIQUES

Put option writing can be applied in the following ways:

For Speculation

Just as a speculator sells call options for a possible price decline in the underlying security, so he sells put options for a possible price rise in the stock.

Buy at Below-Market Price

One could write a put option as a means of acquiring a stock several points below its current market price. Failing that objective, possibly due to a rise in the stock's price, he would be compensated by an earned premium.

Here is an illustration of this method of selling (writing) an option against cash.

Assume that the option writer would like to buy 100

shares of XYZ at 45 instead of paying the current market price of 50. With this in view, he sells a 95-day put option on XYZ at 50 for $550.

Either Earn Premium or Take Stock

If XYZ goes up, the put option will not be exercised, and the option writer will keep the put premium.

On the other hand, if XYZ falls, eventually he will be put 100 shares of XYZ at 50. His effective purchase price of XYZ, however, will not be 50 but 45, as the put premium of $550 he has already earned would reduce the purchase price by that amount.

It is apparent, therefore, that this option writing strategy dictates that put options be written only on stocks that option writers would be willing to own, albeit at a price somewhat below the market.

After the put option is exercised, the writer normally would seek to sell a call option against the stock that he now owns as a result of the put option.

Just as call option writers, put option writers accept market risks on the down side. They take the risk that the stock might go down more than the premium received during the time period of the option contract.

Possible Defenses

What are the possible defenses for put option writers to minimize their exposure? First, there are several ground rules to observe:

1. Sell put options only against cash and only on securities desirable for your portfolio.
2. Use only a fraction of your funds in any single put option writing situation.
3. Place a ceiling on the number of put options sold to

expire in any one month. This spreads risk and evens out fluctuations.

Specifically, there are several defense strategies for the put option writer if the underlying security upon which he has issued a put option has declined in price.

Defense #1
One possible recourse open to the writer who remains bullish about the stock in spite of its price decline is to write a naked call option at the price to which the stock has declined.

Defense #2
Another possible recourse is to sell the stock short at a price to which the stock has declined.

Defense #3
A third possible defense is to sell the stock short at the price to which it has declined and to purchase an above-the-market call at the original strike price for the remaining period of the put option.

This defensive strategy is to limit loss to the premium paid for the above-the-market call, as well as to prevent substantial loss.

Generally, above-the-market call options are available at prices much lower than market options. The option writer can buy a call at the market price of the stock, provided that an above-the-market call is not readily available.

Commissions Difference
While put option writers and call option writers incur about the same risks of a possible stock-price drop, there is quite a difference in commissions for the two kinds of option writers.

Put writers have an opportunity to earn premiums free of expenses if they should prove to be correct in their judgement. They reserve cash, however, to pay for the delivery of the stock should the put option be exercised.

Essentially, put options are sold for a premium profit that would be taxed as a long-term capital gain if such a profit were realized after put contracts have been held for more than six months.

If the market should go against the put option writer, he would not incur any loss until the amount of stock decline exceeds the put premium received.

CHAPTER XI

STRADDLE OPTION STRATEGIES

Option Variations

In addition to puts and calls, there are option variations that can be created by combining the two basic types of options.

While there are a significant number of option variations, straddles and spreads are next only to puts and calls themselves and, together with the first two, constitute the primary forms of contracts in the growing universe of options.

Multiple Combinations

Straddles and spreads are two of the most frequently used multiple option combinations. They come in varying forms of calls and puts.

As a group, multiple combinations are designed mainly to limit risk and enhance profitability

1. within a given price range with maximum profitability at one price in between;
2. at less than one price and more than another.

This chapter and the following, dealing with straddles and spreads respectively, cover some of the important option techniques or strategies from the standpoints both of the buyer and the seller.

Two Separate Options in One

A straddle is a combination of one call and one put written on the same stock at the same striking price with the same expiration date. A straddle consists of two separate option contracts sold for a single price. The exercise of one does not void the remaining contract.

Specifically, a straddle gives the holder (1) the right, at his option, to sell to the maker of the contract the stated number of shares of the specified stock at the stated price before the specified date as well as (2) the right to receive and buy from the maker the stated number of shares of the specified stock at the same price before the same date.

Need Not Know Market Direction

While call buyers and put buyers venture to guess the market direction of a particular stock in a given time period, straddle buyers need not know the direction of the market.

For a straddle buyer to profit from his transaction, he needs only a sufficient fluctuation in the price of the stock, regardless of its direction.

At Best on Volatile Stocks

Straddles work best on volatile stocks due to their likelihood of fluctuation.

Since some movement in one direction or the other is very likely during the life of a straddle, a straddle buyer is highly unlikely to lose his entire straddle premium because one side or the other of a straddle on volatile stocks should have value.

Even by doing nothing till expiration, the chances are

quite good that the holder of a straddle may realize a profit by liquidating its profitable side at the end of the straddle life.

Straddle Premium

Since it would be highly unusual for straddle holders not to liquidate one side of a straddle option profitably, straddle writers generally obtain larger premiums than call or put writers. For the same time period, straddle premiums are approximately 70 percent higher than call premiums.

The relatively higher straddle premium also results from generally high demand for straddles, because option dealers often prepare to position straddles as part of their inventory. The willingness on the part of dealers is due to their general belief that they would have more than an even chance to liquidate one or both portions of straddles profitably.

There are, however, two sides to the coin. The generally higher premiums for straddle options mean correspondingly larger losses should they fail to work out because of lack of movement in normally "move" stocks. Also, an insufficient movement in the price of such stocks would cause straddle buyers to lose the bulk of their premium money.

STRADDLE BUYING STRATEGIES

"Buy-and-Hold" Technique

Since many high-P/E, high-priced stocks, which are more often than not highly volatile ones, fluctuate quite frequently to the extent of 15 percent and 20 percent and, sometimes, considerably more during the life of a 95-day straddle, there is a distinct possibility that profitable liquidation of one portion of the straddle may be realized at expiration just by buying and holding the straddle and doing nothing until such expiration.

Recoup Entire Premium With Half Option

In taking this "buy-and-hold" approach, the straddler hopes for a sufficiently large stock-price fluctuation in either direction to recoup the entire straddle acquisition premium, together with transaction costs, plus a profit.

While it would be highly unusual for high-P/E, high-priced, normally volatile stocks to remain at the same price level for a longer-term option period, straddlers are still exposed to the risk of losing a substantial, if not the entire, amount of straddle premiums.

"Trading Hedge" Technique

For professional straddlers, a trading approach is likely to be more profitable than the above "buy-and-hold" technique. They incline more toward cashing in on short-term trading profits while bulwarking these short-term trades with straddles as a risk-limiting insurance.

In other words, trading straddlers are more interested in a series of short-term trading profits than in a larger gain in one particular market direction.

One Trading Cycle

Assume that you had bought a 95-day straddle on XYZ at 60 for $1,000. If XYZ went up to 70 several weeks later, you might decide to sell 100 shares of XYZ short at 70.

If XYZ went up further before the expiration of the straddle, you would use the call portion of the straddle to cover at 60 your 100-share short position in XYZ.

Now, let us assume further that after your short sale XYZ reversed directions and went down to 64. At this point if you had bought 100 shares of XYZ at 64 to cover short, you would have realized a profit of $600 before commissions, with your original straddle position remaining intact.

Thus, you had completed one trading cycle, both with a profit and still with the same straddle.

Postured for More Trading

Should, then, the purchase of XYZ at 64 have proved to be ill advised, with XYZ moving down to 54, you would have passed up an opportunity to gain another 10 points on the short side.

Other Straddle Half Becoming Effective

At this juncture, however, the put portion of your straddle position became operative. By buying 100 shares of XYZ at 54, you would lock up a six-point gain, being the difference between the then-prevailing market price of 54 and the put strike price of 60.

Once again, it might prove advantageous for you to keep the long position for the possible purpose of trading profitably in the open market.

Protected Short or Long Purchase

The above is illustrative of how traders use a straddle option as a hedge to make protected short sales or long stock purchases after the stock has moved away from the straddle strike price.

"Free-Option" Technique

An even more sophisticated straddle technique is first to recover your straddle cost through exercise of one (either put or call) side of the straddle. Upon recouping your straddle investment early in the straddle life span, you would own the unexercised part of the straddle as a free option. This unused part of the straddle could become valuable if the underlying security subsequently moved back into the straddle life.

"Call" To Sell or "Put" To Buy

Assume that you bought a 95-day straddle position on XYZ at 60 (strike price) at a premium cost of $600. Assume further that you exercised the "call" portion of your straddle right to buy XYZ at $600 when XYZ went up from $60 to $70 several weeks later. On the day you exercised your "call" right, you sold XYZ at $70, locking in the 10-point, or $1,000, profit.

The above purchase (through the exercise of your "call" right and the same-day sale of XYZ) would involve no additional capital under New York Stock Exchange rules.

While our illustrative strategy above involves exercising the "call" right and selling the stock, it could be done the other way around, that is, exercising the "put" right and buying the stock, depending on which direction the stock goes.

Profit "Pyramiding"

Our happy straddler in the above example may choose to pyramid his straddling profits further.

For one thing, with the profit from the "call" right exercised above, he may buy a new straddle on, say, the same XYZ at $60.

If and when XYZ drops from $60 to $50 during the early or middle part of the straddle life, the straddler can now exercise the hitherto unexercised "put" right to put (sell) XYZ at $60 after purchasing XYZ at $50 in the open market, thus locking in another 10-point, or $1,000, profit.

In addition, our straddler retains a free "call" option at $60 that may become valuable if the underlying security should again move back into the remaining straddle life.

Meanwhile, once again the profit from exercising the above "put" right can be used to establish still a further new straddle position if our happy straddler should choose to do so.

Buying Guidelines

The above illustrations give us a number of straddle-buying guidelines:

1. Buy straddles only on volatile stocks.
2. Of volatile stocks, emphasis should be laid on comparatively high-P/E, high-priced stocks to leave enough room for price fluctuations.
3. Buy straddles of no less than 90-day duration. For one thing, shorter-term straddles may not leave sufficient time for the desired price fluctuations to occur. For another, longer-duration straddles as a rule cost less than shorter-term straddles in line with the principle of economy on "volume."
4. Limit the cost of a 95-day straddle premium to a level somewhat below 20 percent of the market price of the underlying security.

STRADDLE WRITING (SELLING) STRATEGIES

Special Tax Advantages

Special tax advantages generally motivate straddlers more into writing (selling) than buying straddles.

To begin with, the premium received from the sale of a straddle is required, under Internal Revenue Service rules, to be apportioned between the call portion and the put portion, with 55 percent and 45 percent, respectively, normally going to the call and to the put.

Many straddlers, however, use the 50-50 ratio of apportioning that is also acceptable to the Internal Revenue Service so long as this apportionment is made consistently.

Uncombined Options

Straddle writers (sellers) enjoy distinct tax-treatment advantages over writers of uncombined (individual) call or put options.

When a single call or put option expires unexercised, the call or put premium received by the writer (seller) becomes ordinary income.

Ordinary Income Versus Short-Term Capital Gain

In sharp contrast to the unfavorable tax treatment of unexercised single call or put options, when one portion of a straddle is exercised the premium received from the unexercised portion becomes a short-term gain to the straddle writer. This gain can be used to offset any short-term or long-term loss that may have been incurred by the straddle writer.

Now, let us proceed to examine a number of straddle writing techniques.

"Naked" Straddle Writing

A speculator may choose to write straddles against cash, which is equivalent to writing "naked" straddles.

When a straddler writes a straddle option against cash, he does not expect the underlying security to fluctuate in either direction by an amount that would exceed the straddle premium he has received.

A "naked" straddle writer normally is prepared to sell additional straddles on the same underlying security at different price intervals, even though no stock has been put to him or called by him.

Bullish Straddle Writing

A straddler with a bullish bias may buy 100 shares of XYZ, say, at $60 and sell a 95-day straddle option for, say, $1,000. This straddle position is tantamount to selling one call option against a long position and one put option against cash.

Should XYZ go up in price to, say, $70, as our straddler had expected, the "call" portion of his straddle position would be exercised. He would have to deliver 100 shares of XYZ at $60, resulting in a 10-point gain to him.

If, on the other hand, XYZ should drop in price to, say, $50, the exercise of the "put" portion of his straddle position would be triggered. In this case our unhappy straddler would be saddled with a second 100 shares of XYZ in addition to his original 100-share position, with the market price of XYZ being somewhere below the straddle strike price of $60.

Either To Sell at Premium or Buy More

It is apparent, therefore, from the above illustration, that when one sells a straddle one is willing either to sell out for the straddle premium received or to buy additional shares of the underlying security.

Note: In setting up a straddle, the straddler will be required to put up margin against the put side although his "long" stock position will cover the "call" side of the straddle.

The above illustration involves the exercise of only one side of a straddle position.

Ordinarily Only One-Sided Exercise

Since the bulk of straddle writings have ended with exercise of only one side (either "call" or "put") of the straddle position, writers will more often than not find themselves "put" with additional stock and be faced with the necessity to seek opportunities to write additional straddles or calls on both their original stock position and their newly acquired (put) stock.

Rare Exercise of Both Sides

While it is only very rarely, indeed, that both sides of a straddle would be exercised against the straddle writer, it remains a possibility. It happens when XYZ may fluctuate widely enough to bring into life, first, one side of the straddle, and then the other side, all during the time period of the option.

In that very unlikely event, the straddler would be left with 100 shares of XYZ and, in our above illustration, $1,000 in straddle premium before commissions. The extent of his profit or loss would be determined by the market value of XYZ prevailing at that time.

Bearish Straddle Writing

Straddlers with a bearish bias may choose to write straddles against short positions. A bearish straddle writer seeks to earn a premium profit in accordance with his negative view that the stock underlying the straddle position will decline in price during the life of the straddle. Should his negative assessment of the underlying security prove correct, he would be "put" the stock through the exercise of the "put" side by the straddle buyer.

Offsetting "Short" Position

To protect himself against this likely "put" prospect, the straddler executes an offsetting "short" position that would be closed out with the stock that might be "put" to him. For our bearish straddler to earn a profit, the straddle premium would have to be sufficiently large to exceed the transaction costs in shorting and buying the stock.

CHAPTER XII

OPTION SPREADING

Spread—Another Combination Option

A spread is similar to a straddle—a combination of a put and a call—except that where a straddle is a combination of a put option and a call option at the same price, a spread normally is a put option at a price below the current market price of the underlying security, and a call option above the market price of the underlying security.

In other words, a conventional spread is "long" on the option with a striking price higher than the market price, but "short" on the option with a striking price lower than the market price.

Two Options in One

Similar to straddles, spreads are actually two separate option contracts in one. While composed of two distinctly individual options, a spread option order cannot be executed unless both sides of the order are executed. This is because the two-orders-in-one are in fact entered as a unit order.

Premium Cost Comparisons

Generally, a spread costs less in premium than a straddle because of its relatively lower risk to the seller.

Normally, the seller prefers selling a straddle for more cash. However, the major advantage in selling a spread is this: if, at the expiration of the spread, the underlying security that was selling, say, at 40 at the time of structuring that spread is now selling between 39 and 41, the chances are that neither the put option nor the call option is likely to be exercised.

On the other hand, if a straddle at 50 was sold, the chances are greater that at least one side of the straddle, if not both, will be exercised.

In his *Understanding Put and Call Options*, which was first published in 1959, Herbert Filer, a leading pioneer of stock market options, made a highly revealing cost comparison of spreads with straddles in these words:

> The Spread is less expensive than a Straddle on the same stock for the same length of time by approximately half the difference of the spread between the Put and Call. For example, if a Straddle at 60 were to cost $600, a Spread of two points up and two points down would cost $400. The difference of $200 would represent half of the spread between 58 and 62.

Straddle at 60——cost $600
Spread 58–62——cost $400

Basic Concepts

The concept of spreads was borrowed from the commodity futures markets and adapted to listed options. Essentially, spreads are an application of the century-old arbitrage technique to the field of options, utilizing the basic concepts of price differentials and time dissipation of premium.

Spread Premiums

A spread is the dollar difference between the buy and sell premiums. Its object is to capture the difference in premiums between the "long" option and the "short" option. A spreader is concerned with the extent of spread between the premium paid and the premium received in establishing the spread position. The prices at which the spread order is executed are no concern to him.

Spreads in "Debit"

If the cost of the "long" option is more than the "short" option, the spread is expressed as a "debit."

To illustrate, if you had made a "spread" on Eastman Kodak (NYSE-99⅛-EK) by buying an EK October 90 option at 13¾ and selling EK October 100 at 8½ (based on June 17, 1975, closing prices), you would have been 5¼ points in "debit" as follows:

Buy EK October 90 at 13¾
Sell EK October 100 at 8½
$$\overline{\phantom{\text{Sell EK October 100 at }}}$$
Debit   5¼

The debit resulted from the fact that you were "long" the more expensive option and "short" the less expensive option.

Spreads in "Credit"

Reversely, if the cost of the "long" option is less than the "short" option, the spread is expressed as a "credit."

As an illustration, if you had made a "spread" on Avon Products (NYSE-31¼-AVP) by buying AVP April 30 at 3⅞ and selling AVP April 20 at 11¼ (based on January 27, 1975, closing prices), you would have been 7⅜ points in "credit" as follows:

Sell AVP April 20 at 11¼
Buy AVP April 30 at 3⅞
_____
            Credit   7⅜

This credit resulted from the fact that you were "short" the more expensive option and "long" the less expensive option.

"Even" Spread
If the cost of the "long" option equals the cost of the "short" option, the spread is said to be "even."

Spread Margins
Before the advent of new rules for listed options, option margin rules were based on the notion that "shorting" calls was extremely risky. To effectuate a "spread" on IBM, for example, would be a very-high-margin-requirement proposition.

Changed Margin Requirements
Under new margin requirements regarding hedging of listed options, the "long" option under certain conditions is considered adequate margin for the short position.

As a result of the changed margin requirements for spreads, the leverage for call-backed-call optioning and that for stock-backed-call writing has considerably widened, as illustrated by the following example.

Call-Backed Call Versus Stock-Backed Call
This example is based on a comparison of writing an October 40 call at 6½ backed by 100 shares of Honeywell (NYSE-39¾-HON) versus the same call backed by an October 30 call bought at 12⅜.

In the stock-backed call, cash layout on a 50-percent margin and after premium deduction of 6½ was $1,337.50, as follows:

Buy 100 HON at	$3,975.00
50% Margin	1,987.50
	$1,987.50
Less Premium	650.00
Cash Layout	$1,337.50

On the other hand, in the call-backed call, the cash outlay after premium deduction is 5⅞, as follows:

Buy HON Oct. 30 at	$1,237.50
Sell HON Oct. 40 at	650.00
Cash Layout	$ 587.50

The call-backed-call leverage was well over two to one compared with the stock-backed-call leverage.

Different Margin Requirements

Different margin requirements cover bull spreads and bear spreads.

Essentially, a bullish spread is "long" the more expensive option and "short" the less expensive option.

Conversely, a bearish spread is "long" the less expensive option and "short" the more expensive option.

Bull Spread Margins

The new margin requirements can be summarized as follows:

The short position is considered covered provided that

the long position, which must be paid for, (1) has the *same* or *lower striking* price than the short position, and (2) has the *same* or *later expiration* date than the short position.

As illustrations we use Disney options of different expiration months and different striking prices (based on July 11, 1975, closing prices), as follows:

		July	*October*	*January*
Disney	60	3/16	3⅜	5¼
Disney	50	4⅛	7⅝	9¾
Disney	45	8⅝	11	12¾

Note: Disney (DIS) closed at 53⅜ on July 11, 1975.

1. Different Striking Prices
(A) Same Expiration Month
Illustration #1: When the "long" position has the same expiration month as the short position:

        Buy DIS January 50 at 9¾
        Sell DIS January 60 at <u>5¼</u>
        Margin requirement   4½

(B) Later Expiration Month
Illustration #2: When the long position has a later expiration month than the short position:

        Buy DIS January 60 at 5¼
        Sell DIS October 60 at <u>3⅜</u>
        Margin requirement   1⅞

2. Different Expiration Months
(A) Same Strike Price
Illustration #3: When the long position has the same striking price as the short position (the

144

above example in Illustration #2 is also applicable here):

Buy DIS January 60 at 5¼
Sell DIS October 60 at 3⅜
Margin requirement   1⅞

(B) Lower Strike Price
Illustration #4: When the long position has a lower striking than the short position:

Buy DIS October 45 at   11
Sell DIS July 50 at   4⅛
Margin requirement   6⅞

Bear Spread Margins
If one buys higher striking price and sells the lower striking price (a bearish spread), the margin requirement will be the differential between *striking prices plus* the "long" option premium, *less* the "short" option premium.

Illustration #1: Illustrative of the above requirement was the following example (based on January 27, 1975, closing prices of Upjohn).

If you had bought UPJ July 50 at 2⅛ and sold UPJ July 45 at 3⅛, the requirement would have been $500 (striking price differential), plus 2⅛ ("long" option premium), less 3⅛ ("short" option premium), as follows:

Striking Price Differential $500.00
Plus "Long" Option Premium   212.50
                                          $712.50
Less "Short" Option Premium   312.50
                                          $400.00

Illustration #2: Also illustrative of bear spread margin requirements was the following example (based on January 27, 1975, closing prices):

If you had bought UPJ October 50 at 3⅜ and sold UPJ October 40 at 5¾, the margin requirement was $1,000 (striking price differential), plus 3⅜ ("long" option premium), less 5¾ ("short" option premium), as follows:

Striking Price Differential	$1,000.00
Plus "Long" Option Premium	337.50
	$1,337.50
Less "Short" Option Premium	575.00
	$ 762.50

Illustration #3: Also illustrative of the margin requirement of another "bear spread" (buying higher striking price and selling lower striking price with the same expiration month) was the following example (based on January 27, 1975, closing prices).

If you had bought an April 30 option of Avon Products (NYSE-31¼-AVP) at 3⅞ and sold AVP April 20 at 11¼, the margin requirement would have been $1,000 (striking price differential), plus 3⅞ ("long" option premium), less 11¼ ("short" option premium), as follows:

146

Striking Price Differential	$1,000
Plus "Long" Option Premium	387.50
	$1,387.50
Less "Short" Option Premium	1,125.00
	$ 262.50

Anatomy of a Bear Spread

The above "bear spread" example on Avon Products provides an anatomy of what could happen to the spreader in terms of profit or loss, if Avon (1) goes down to 20 or less or (2) stays within the "spread" range (between 20 and 30); or (3) rises to 30 or higher.

A. If Avon goes down to 20 or less?
Profit is $737.50 (11¼ less 3⅞), since both options are worthless, plus you still retain $262.50 margin deposit.

B. If Avon stays within range of 20 and 30?
Spread could narrow. Profit would be difference of new spread and 7⅜.

C. If Avon rises to 30 or higher?
Maximum loss is $262.50, which is the difference between the two striking prices (20–30) less the credit differential of $737.50

At a premium cost of $262.50, the above spreader on Avon would risk a maximum $262.50 to make $737.50 in the three months between January 27, 1975, and the end of April 1975.

147

Low-Risk Option Vehicle

The risk of a spread, whether it be bearish or bullish, is limited to the amount of the spreader's premium money plus his entry and exit costs.

Together with covered writing, spreads are considered relatively low-risk option vehicles. The cost of spreading (call-backed call) is relatively modest versus that for covered writing (stock-backed call), a comparison of which was made earlier in this chapter.

For a bear, a "bearish" spread provides him with a vehicle of limited potential loss instead of selling (shorting) an option "naked," without owning the underlying shares.

CHAPTER XIII

SPREAD TECHNIQUES (HORIZONTAL)

Various Spread Techniques

A whole array of spread techniques are available for sophisticated investors, depending on their investment and hedging objectives, as well as on their view of market trends and of particular underlying stocks.

Despite the differences in their makeup, the various spreads have something basic in common, as all of them consist of simultaneously buying and selling options on the same stock, with different strike prices and/or different expiration months.

"Simultaneous" Long and Short

Thus, despite their varying construction, all forms of spreading have at least one thing in common: that is, they contain "simultaneous" long and short positions.

The two principal forms of spread techniques are the horizontal spread and the vertical spread.

Horizontal Spread

Also called "calendar" or "time" spread, a horizontal spread is the purchase of a listed option and the sale of a listed option having the same exercise price but different expiration months. A horizontal spread is considered a relatively conservative option approach.

Vertical Spread

Also called "money" or "price" spread, a vertical spread is the purchase of a listed option and the sale of a listed option having the same expiration month but different striking prices.

Diagonal Spread

A diagonal spread is the purchase of a listed option and the sale of a listed option combining different striking prices and different expiration months.

Sandwich Spread

Also known as a "butterfly," a sandwich spread consists of the sale of two intermediate listed options and the purchase of two listed options with striking prices being of equal distance from the short calls in the ratio of 1:2:1.

If the long calls are not of equal distance, there will be additional risk exposure.

Bull Horizontal and Bear Horizontal

Just as with other spread forms, horizontal spreads consist of two kinds: bull horizontal spreads and bear horizontal spreads.

Bull horizontals are designed to exploit changes in relative premiums, from a bullish situation, with spreads on different expiration months but with the same striking price. In bull horizontals, you long the more-distant-expiration-month option and short the nearby-month-expiration option. The more-distant-month option invariably costs more in option premium than the closer-by-month option.

Bear horizontals are designed to generate a cash flow return, from a bearish situation, on spreads of different expiration months but of the same striking price. In bear horizontals, you long the nearby-month expiration and short the more-distant-month expiration.

The point difference in time spreads will usually be greatest if the underlying stock is selling at or near the exercise price shortly before the expiration of the near-term option.

Higher-Potential Spread Opportunities

Higher-potential spread opportunities generally exist in situations where the purchased contract has a more-distant expiration month than the one sold.

Small-Capital-Expenditure Vehicle

Under the new rules on margin requirements on spreads, the long option is deemed adequate to cover the short option. As a result, an investor need only put up the difference between the prices of two options. The new margin requirements have made spreads a small-capital-expenditure vehicle and one of the more attractive option possibilities for investors.

How To Select Stocks for Spreads

The potentially most promising spreads are those of relatively volatile stocks with a small spread premium differential between two options.

Among others, the following are several important pointers for time spreading:

Relative Volatility

While some degree of volatility is desirable for time spreading, avoid positioning time spreads where the underlying security could advance or decline from the strike price by more than 50 percent for a stock under 50, 30 percent for a stock between 50 and 100, and 25 percent for a stock over 100.

Small Spread Premium

A narrow spread premium differential is prerequisite to time spreading. Spread premium differential is that between the premium you pay for the long position and the premium you received for the short position.

Also, avoid positioning a time spread if the option premium on the long position is less than 10 percent of the price of the underlying security.

Striking Price

Generally you should avoid positioning a time spread when the striking price is at that point substantially below the price of the underlying security.

In the selection of a striking price for time spreading after a major market decline, it is generally more desirable to select one that is above the then market price of the underlying security.

Spreading Profit Versus Near-Term Expiration

A spreader will probably have made the bulk of his profit when the market price of the underlying security is close to the striking price with approximately one month remaining in the life of the near-term option. Avoid waiting until the very end of the near-term option to take spreading profit.

Low-Cost "Long" Call
At the expiration of the near-term option, you will be left with a "long" call at a very low cost if the underlying security is trading at or near the striking price.

Multiple Options
It would help enhance the possibility of spread profits if you start by reducing per-option commission costs through doing spreads in quantities. Since commission costs are heavy in setting up spreads, it would be advisable to do them in multiples of five to ten. One possible approach: do no fewer than ten calls for spreads under $1; no fewer than five calls for spreads between $1 and $3; no fewer than three calls for spreads over $3.

Spread Risks
The following is a highly revealing capsule summary of spread risks, according to the CBOE:

> While the benefits of spreading are often readily apparent, some of the limitations and risks may be somewhat less visible. Some considerations which are unique to spreads should be weighed before entering a spread position.
>
> a). Spread orders are relatively difficult to execute.
> b). Early exercise could destroy a spread. If the short side of a spread is exercised, a whole new set of cir-

cumstances arise. If spreaders aren't prepared for an early call, they might have to exercise a long call which has a significant premium.

c). Lifting a leg of the spread can significantly increase risk. Anyone lifting a leg on a spread should recognize the greatly increased exposure to market fluctuations.

d). Tax consequences could make a successful spread unprofitable. A potential spread might indicate a low-risk position with a potential profit on the short side which could be larger than the loss on the long side. However, if both sides are to be closed out or allowed to expire, the tax consequence would diminish any profit.

Historical Premium-Differential Relationships

Below is an illustration of how to exploit the present option premium differential versus its historical premium differential.

A horizontal spread could be structured on IBM (NYSE-203½) June 17, 1975, by sale of a nearer-term option to reduce the cost of a more-distant-term option, as follows:

Buy IBM January 200 at   28
Sell IBM October 200 at   21¼
                         ―――――
          Debit   6¾

Historically, the premium differential between an intermediate-term IBM option and a far-term IBM option with three months separating them was wider than the premium debit of 6¾ indicated in this spread.

The spreader's possible profit was predicated upon a

possible widening of the premium spread of 6¾.

Low-Cost Spreads on Fluctuating Stocks

While narrow premium spreads are generally available on stable stocks, they don't come too often on volatile stocks normally fluctuating over a wide zone.

A low-cost option spread on a widely moving stock was found available on May 5, 1975, on Homestake (NYSE-44¾-HM) which would involve the purchase of a HM October 50 call at 4½ and the sale of a HM July 50 at 3, with a 1½ point debit.

Since the long position had a later expiration month than the short position, the short position was considered covered. Requirement was $150 (4½ less 3). The maximum loss would be limited to $150 (the premium differential) plus commissions.

HM had been fluctuating in a wide band for over nine months, with a recent trading range of 40–49.

Spread Widening with Near-Term Expiration

The following two spreads are illustrative of spreads widening as near-expiration premiums drop:

One was the possible purchase on February 24, 1975, of a July 80 option at 8¾ on Xerox (NYSE-78⅝-XRX) and the sale of XRX April 80 at 5⅜, with a 3⅜ debit, as follows:

Buy July 80   8¾
Sell April 80 5⅜
          ———
    Debit   3⅜

As XRX April 80s draw close to expiration, their premium would drop, probably widening the spread to five, or perhaps six, points.

The other situation would involve the purchase on February 14, 1975, of a July 70 option at 13¼, also on Xerox, and the sale of XRX April 70 at 10⅞, with a 2⅜-point debit, as follows:

Buy XRX July 70   13¼
Sell XRX April 70 10⅞
_____
Debit   2⅜

As XRX April 70 draws toward expiration, its premium will drop, widening the spread probably to four or five points.

Exploiting Expiration-Time Tool

Generally the horizontal spread can serve as an instrument of exploiting the near-term-expiration option as its expiration time draws near.

The most propitious time for expiration-time exploitation occurs when the upside visibility of the underlying security beyond the striking price is not that clear and when the near-term out of the money option is still carrying a large premium.

Illustrative of expiration-time exploitation was the possible purchase on March 28, 1975, of a July 50 option (far-term) at 4⅜ on Philip Morris (NYSE-48¾-MO) and the sale of MO April 50 (near-term) at 1 13/16, as follows:

Buy MO July 50 at   4⅜
Sell MO April 50 at 1 13/16
_____
Debit   2 9/16

Double-Edged Strategy

Such a horizontal spread can serve double-edged purposes.

Should the underlying security rise above the strike price, the near-term option might be selling at only slightly more than the earlier price, because in the money near-term options, as a rule, lose whatever premium over intrinsic value they may be carrying.

At this point, the spreader could buy back the near-term option at a price probably not appreciably higher than the price originally sold for.

More Expensive Option at Reduced Risk

The upshot of the above is that the spreader would be able to carry a more expensive option at reduced cost and, therefore, with reduced risks.

Should the underlying security fail to go beyond the striking price, the near-term option would become worthless. In that case, the spreader would use the option premium received from the near-term option to reduce the cost of his distant-month option.

How To Reduce Spread Cost to Zero

To further illustrate the above strategy was a possible spread on Proctor and Gamble (NYSE-PG) which closed at 96 for the week ending March 28, 1975.

If you had sold one PG April 90 option at 6½ and, simultaneously, bought one PG July 90 option at 9¾, you would have had a debit of 3¼ points, as follows:

Buy PG July 90 at   9¾
Sell PG April 90 at 6½
_____

    Debit   3¼

If, at the end of April, PG sold at 90 or slightly below, the April 90 call you had sold short would be worthless, but the July 90 call might be selling around 6 or 6½ for a potential good profit if sold.

Or, alternately, you could then sell a higher-strike option (PG July 100) around 3¼, which would reduce your cost on the July 90 call to zero.

Below-Intrinsic-Value Options

Spreaders should be aware of spreading risks involving "deep in the money" options selling at below their intrinsic value.

Illustrative of the above was what would be a bad spread on March 12, 1975, involving the purchase of a July 30 option at 8¾ on Alcoa (NYSE-37½-AA) and the sale of an AA April 30 option at 7¼, as follows:

Buy AA July 30 at 8¾
Sell AA April 30 at 7¼

_____

Debit   1½

Since AA April 30 at 7¼ was ¼ point below the intrinsic value (7¼ plus the striking price at 30, totaling 37¼, or ¼ below the market price of 37½), a spread involving such "deep in the money" options as the short position should be avoided.

Possible Early Exercise

Spreading involving such "deep in the money" options runs the further risk of possible early exercise of the options. In that event, the spreader would incur commission expenses in purchasing and selling the required number of shares of the underlying security.

158

Only Useful to Arbitrageurs

Such below-intrinsic-value options are useful only to professional arbitrageurs who could execute a "simultaneous" transaction by purchasing the underlying security at 37½ and exercising the call option at 7¼, thereby earning a comparatively risk-free one-eighth or one-quarter point.

RATIO SPREADING

Whole Range of Possibilities

Just as ratio writing comes in varying forms, so ratio spreading covers a whole range of possibilities, including using different striking prices, or different expiration months, or a combination of different striking prices *and* different expiration months.

Illustration—Using Different Striking Prices

To illustrate one of the most frequently used forms of ratio spreading, we use the purchase of one option and the sale of two or more options of the same stock, having different striking prices, but the same expiration month, as follows:

Assuming that XYZ July 60 is trading at 5 and XYZ July 70 at 2, with common being quoted at 58:

Buy 1 XYZ July 60 at $500
Sell 3 XYZ July 70 (at $200) $600
                                            ———
    Credit $100

Risk and Profit Potential

In the event that the option premiums trade at their intrinsic value at expiration, the risk and profit potential would be as follows:

Downside risk	zero
Upside risk	75½
Maximum Profit Point	70

Since XYZ at 58 has about 30 percent before rising above 75½ at expiration, the spread is profitable.

If XYZ trades at 70 at any time near the end of the option period, then the 60 call is worth about 10 while the 70 call approximates zero in value. The profit to the spreader is approximately $1,100 ($1,000+$600−$500).

Two-Against-One Ratio Spreading

Instead of the above three-against-one ratio spreading, we also can construct a two-against-one ratio spreading, as illustrated below:

When Xerox was trading at 76¾, its April 70 option and April 80 option were worth 11 and 5⅛, respectively.

A possible ratio spread of one long call (April 70 at 11) against two short calls (April 80 at 5⅛ each) could be structured as follows:

Buy 1 XRX April 70 at	11
Sell 2 XRX April 80 (at 5⅛ each)	10¼
Debit	¾

Reverse Horizontal Hedge

Ratio spreading that involves the purchase of two near-term options and the sale of one far-term option of the same striking price is also called a reverse horizontal hedge.

160

Structurally, a reverse horizontal hedge is essentially as follows:

Buy two XYZ July 30
Sell one XYZ Oct. 30

One of the primary purposes of this spread construction is to develop a free call with a hedge.

CHAPTER XIV

SPREAD TECHNIQUES (VERTICAL)

Bull Vertical Versus Bear Vertical

Like other forms of spreading techniques, vertical spreads consist of two kinds: bull vertical and bear vertical.

Bull verticals are designed to exploit changes in the price of the underlying security. This objective is generally achieved by buying the lower-striking-price option and selling (shorting) the higher-striking-price option.

Bear verticals are designed to exploit changes in relative premiums. The objective is generally achieved by buying the higher-striking-price option and selling (shorting) the lower-striking-price option.

BULL VERTICAL SPREAD TECHNIQUES

Profit Made on Upside

Also known as bull perpendicular spreads, bull vertical spreads involve buying low-strike options and selling high-strike options, for the same time period. Profit is made on the upside.

The key to successful bull spreading is finding situations with narrow premium spreads.

Low-Cost Bull Perpendicular Spreads

An interesting bull perpendicular spread on June 13,

162

1975, on Deere (NYSE-41-DE) involved the purchase of 10 DE October 40 calls and the sale of 10 DE October 45 calls, with a premium spread for 2¼ (plus ⅛ discretion), as structured below:

Buy 10 DE October 40

Spread for 2¼ (plus ⅛ dis.)

Sell 10 DE October 45

Stock must move to 45 to reach maximum profit potential.

At 45: October 45's are worth 0

October 40's are worth 5, for a profit of $2,625

Breakeven point for this trade is DE at 42½ at expiration date.

On June 17, 1975, another bull perpendicular spread on Deere, then available at 39½, could be constructed as follows:

Buy DE October 40 at 4
Sell DE October 45 at 2
                       ──
    Debit   2

The maximum profit potential for this bull spread would be obtainable with DE moving up to 45.

Technically, DE was undergoing correction of recent upswings.

73.8-percent Return in 18 Weeks

Another bull perpendicular spread appeared attractive

163

on June 17, 1975, on Eastman Kodak (NYSE-99⅛-EK) as follows:

Buy EK October 90 at 13¾
Sell EK October 100 at 8½
_____

Debit   5¼

A net cash flow of only $525 would control a $99 stock for 18 weeks.

If EK remained at 99⅛ at expiration, the return would be 73.8 percent in that time span.

Discount Instead of Premium

Probably one of the best risk-reduction option techniques is to buy discount instead of premium.

As a group, spreads provide a fertile field for discount purchases. The following are illustrative of such discounts:

One was a vertical spread on June 3, 1975, on General Electric (NYSE-47⅜-GE) when you could buy the July 45 call for 4⅛ and sell the July 50 call for 1 15/16, with a premium difference of 2 3/16.

Since the July 45 call had an intrinsic value of 2⅜, you actually would obtain a discount of 3/16 instead of paying premium for the spread.

Discount Spreads

Also illustrative of discount spreads was a possible spread on June 3, 1975, on Johnson & Johnson (NYSE-96-JNJ) when you could buy the July 90 call for 9⅛ and sell the July 100 call for 3¾, with a premium difference of 5⅜ points.

Since the July 90 option had an intrinsic worth of 6 points, the spreader actually would obtain ⅝ point in dis-

164

count instead of paying a premium on the spread.

Also Trading Vehicle

Since spreads fluctuate with the price of the underlying security, they also constitute a trading vehicle for sophisticated investors.

On March 28, 1975, a bull spread was feasible on Minnesota Mining (NYSE-MMM) when you could buy MMM October 35 for 5½ and sell MMM October 55 for 4 for a spread of 1½, as follows:

Buy MMM October 35 at 5½
Sell MMM October 55 at 4
_____
1½

MMM is known for its relatively wide-fluctuating movements.

Other Vertical Illustrations

On June 3, 1975, another pair of bull verticals were feasible: one on Upjohn (NYSE-47⅜-UPJ) and the other on Black & Decker (NYSE-35⅞-BDK).

The UPJ vertical would involve the purchase of UPJ July 45 for 4⅞ and the sale of UPJ July 50 for 2½, with a premium difference of 2⅜, with a ⅛ discretion, as follows:

Buy UPJ July 45 at 4⅞
Sell UPJ July 50 at 2½
_____
Debit   2⅜

If the stock rises to 50, the spreader would realize 2⅝ points or 110.5 percent on the invested premium cost in seven weeks.

UPJ's technical pattern was favorable despite its edging toward the next obstacle of 48–53 supply.

The BDK spread would be one where you could buy BDK October 35 for 5⅜ and simultaneously sell BDK October 40 for 3½, with a premium difference of 1⅞, as follows:

Buy BDK October 35 for 5⅜
Sell BDK October 40 for 3½
                            ————
Debit   1⅞

Buy Low-Strike—Sell High-Strike

The importance of doing low-cost bull vertical spreads can not be overly emphasized. Bull vertical spreads involve buying low-strike options and selling high-strike options.

On April 21, 1975, the July 35 and July 40 options on Chase Manhattan (NYSE-33¼-CMB) provided an opportunity for a "strike differential" spread. CMB had experienced an earnings recovery in recent quarters. While banks' extremely wide yield-cost spreads were unlikely to last, spreads were expected to be wider in the next few years than they had been in the recent past.

CMB's then P/E of 5 was one of the lowest among major money-center banks, as compared with its own ten-year average P/E ratio of 11.5.

A bullish spread on CMB's July 35 and July 40 options would involve the purchase of the low strike at 2⅛ and the sale of the high strike at ⅞, with a 1¼-point debit, as follows:

Buy CMB July 35 at 2⅛
Sell CMB July 40 at ⅞
                        ————
Debit   1¼

166

With CMB at 35 or lower at expiration, the maximum loss would be limited to the $125 in premium differential, plus commissions.

The maximum profit occurs when CMB sells at 40 or higher, in which case the gain would be $375 or a 300-percent return on the invested $125, the required cash under the changed margin rules.

Other Examples of Interesting Spreads

Other interesting spread examples were the following situations available on April 23, 1975:

1. *General Telephone & Electronics (GTE)*
   Buy GTE July 20 at 1.5625
   Sell GTE July 25 at   .4375
   _____
   Debit   1.1250

   Maximum gain—3.875
   Maximum loss—1.125

2. *Minnesota Mining (MMM)*
   Buy MMM July 55 at 5.375
   Sell MMM July 65 at 2.000
   _____
   Debit   3.375

   Maximum gain—6.625
   Maximum loss—3.375

BEAR VERTICAL SPREAD TECHNIQUES

Buy High-Strike—Sell Low-Strike

Being the reverse of bull vertical spreads, bear vertical spreads involve buying higher-strike options and selling (shorting) lower-strike options.

The purpose of a bear vertical is to receive the profit from a large decline in the price of the underlying security, as the best profit comes if both options expire worthless. Its profit is made on the downside.

Different Margin Requirement

The margin requirement for bear spreads is different from that for bull spreads because a bear spread is "long" the cheaper option and "short" the more expensive one. The required margin is equal to the difference between striking prices minus premium differential.

Method of Calculating Margin

Illustrative of the method of calculating margin requirements on bear verticals was a possible bear vertical spread on Upjohn (NYSE-37½-UPJ) on February 14, 1975, that would involve the possible purchase of a UPJ July 40 call at 4½ and the sale of UPJ July 30 at 9¾, with a premium differential of 5¼ on the credit side, as follows:

Buy UPJ July 40 at 4½
Sell UPJ July 30 at 9¾

    Credit   5¼

The striking price differential between UPJ July 40 and UPJ July 30 was 10 points.

Since the spreader took in 5¼ points ("long" the cheaper option and "short" the more expensive option), the margin requirement of this spread was based on the following calculation:

Striking Price Differential	10
(less) Premium Differential	5¼
Margin Requirement	4¾

In other words, the option premium differential of $525 was applied toward reducing the margin requirement to $475, which would also be the limit to the spreader's loss.

Another Margin Calculation Illustration

Also illustrative of margin calculations for bear verticals was the possible spread on Burroughs (NYSE-BGH) on March 7, 1975, when you could sell BGH July 80 at 19¾ and buy BGH July 90 at 12⅝, with a premium differential of 7⅛ on the credit side, as follows:

Sell BGH July 80 at	19¾
Buy BGH July 90 at	12⅝
Credit	7⅛

The striking price differential between July 90 and July 80 was 10 points.

To calculate margin requirement for this BGH bear vertical:

Striking Price Differential	10
(less) Premium Differential	7⅛
Margin Requirement	2⅞

169

Striking Prices Relative to Premiums

Generally, in bear verticals, the lower-striking-price option sold by the spreader is usually somewhat in the money while the higher-striking-price option bought is usually somewhat out of the money.

In the illustration on Upjohn, for example, the UPJ July 30 option (lower-strike) sold was "in the money" relative to UPJ common at 37½. On the other hand, the UPJ July 40 (higher-strike) bought was "out of the money" relative to the price of the underlying security.

Bear Vertical Illustrations

The following possible bear verticals appeared attractive on April 18, 1975, and constitute additional examples of such spreads for illustrative purposes:

1. *Bear Vertical on IBM*
    (A) *Premium Differential:*
        Sell IBM July 180 at 38½
        Buy IBM July 200 at 22
        _____
        16½

    (B) *Striking Price Differential:*
        IBM July 200
        IBM July 180
        _____
        20

    (C) *Margin Requirement:*
        Striking Price Differential 20
        Premium Differential   16½
        _____
        3½

170

(D) Maximum gain 16½
    Maximum loss 3½

2. *Bear Vertical on Texas Instruments (TXN)*
   (A) Premium Differential:
      Sell TXN October 80 at 34
      Buy TXN October 90 at 24¾
      _____
                    9¼

   (B) Striking Price Differential:
      TXN October 90
      TXN October 80
      _____
                 10

   (C) Margin Requirement:
      Striking Price Differential 10
      Premium Differential   9¼
      _____
                    ¾

   *(D) Maximum gain 9¼
       Maximum loss ¾

3. *Bear Vertical on McDonald (MCD)*
   (A) Premium Differential:
      Sell MCD July 40 at 10
      Buy MCD July 45 at 6¾
      _____
                    3¼

(*B*) *Striking Price Differential:*

MCD July	45
MCD July	40
	5

(*C*) *Margin Requirement:*

Striking Price Differential	5
Premium Differential	3¼
	1¾

(*D*) Maximum gain 3¼
Maximum loss 1¾

4. *Bear Vertical on General Electric (GE)*

(*A*) *Premium Differential:*

Sell GE July 35 at	13
Buy GE July 40 at	7⅜
	5⅝

(*B*) *Striking Price Differential:*

GE July	40
GE July	35
	5

(*C*) *Margin Requirement:*

Striking Price Differential	5
Premium Differential	5⅝
	(⅝)

(*D*) Maximum gain 5⅝
Maximum loss zero

Key Measurements

Option strategy is determined by the follow[ing] considerations:

1. Premium Differential (PD) represents the maximum potential, being the difference between the more expensive low-strike option price and the less expensive high-strike option price.
2. Maximum Loss (ML) represents Option Capital (OC), which is equal to the differential between the two striking prices less Premium Differential (PD).
3. Profit-Loss Differential (PLD) represents the differential between Premium Differential (PD) and Maximum Loss (ML).
4. Profit Leverage (PL) represents the magnitude of gain, measured by Profit-Loss Differential (PLD) as a percentage of Option Capital (same as ML).
5. Downside Breakeven (DB)
6. Downside Breakeven Percentage (DBP)

Possible Workout Against Key Measurements

The following is a summary of possible workout against key measurements on a package of three stocks to be detailed below:

	Prem. Diff. (PD)	Max. Loss (ML)	Prof.-Loss Diff. (PLD)	Prof. Levge. (PL)
McDonald	$650	$350	$300	86%
Polaroid	$337	$163	$174	107%
Disney	$587	$413	$174	42%

MCDONALD (MCD)
2/24/75

Stock price = 41⅛

Option prices: MCD July 30 = 12⅞
                 MCD July 40 = 6⅜

Option Strategy

Sell MCD July 30	12⅞
Buy MCD July 40	6⅜
PD	6½

Margin requirement (option capital) =
$1,000 − $650 = $350.

Option Worksheet
(1) Premium Differential (PD) = $650
(2) Option Capital (OC) = $350
(3) Maximum Loss (ML) = $350
(4) Profit-Loss Differential (PLD) = $300
(5) Profit Leverage (PL) = 86%

POLAROID (PRD)
2/24/75

Stock price = 20¾

Option prices: PRD April 15 = 6¼
                 PRD April 20 = 2⅞

Option Strategy

Sell PRD April 15	6¼
Buy PRD April 20	2⅞
PD	3⅜

Margin requirement = $500 − $337 = $163

174

Option Worksheet

    (1) Premium Differential (PD)=$337

    (2) Option Capital (OC)=$163

    (3) Maximum Loss (ML)=$163

    (4) Profit-Loss Differential (PLD)=$174

    (5) Profit Leverage (PL)=107%

DISNEY (DIS)
2/24/75

Stock price=39¾

Option prices: DIS July 30=11¾

                    DIS July 40=5⅞

Option Strategy

Sell DIS July 30	11¾
Buy DIS July 40	5⅞
PD	5⅞

Margin requirement=$1,000−$587=$413.

Option Worksheet

    (1) Premium Differential (PD)=$587

    (2) Option Capital (OC)=$413

    (3) Maximum Loss (ML)=$413

    (4) Profit-Loss Differential (PLD)=$174

    (5) Profit Leverage (PL)=42%

SANDWICH SPREADS

With its risk known in advance a sandwich is also designed for accounts that seek protected-gain opportunities, if the stock goes up higher than expected or declines more than anticipated.

Multiple Option Structure

Structurally, a sandwich spread consists of sale of two intermediate calls in the middle and purchase of two calls with strike prices being equidistant from the short calls in a ratio of 1:2:1. If the long calls are not of equal distance, there will be additional risk exposure.

Financial Leverage

Ideally, the sale of two intermediate strike calls will finance the purchase of the long calls. In other words, the cash received from the middle strike calls equals, or nearly so, the cash spent to purchase the long calls. A small cash difference, however, does not eliminate opportunity.

The profit potential can be calculated in advance. While moderate, the gain per dollar of cash investment is potentially enormous percentagewise.

Key Considerations

1. Option Capital (OC) represents the differential between the negative (debit) spread and the positive (credit) spread.
2. Common Strike Differential (CSD).
3. Potential Profit (PP) represents the difference between CSD and OC.

For quickly evaluating sandwich spreads, take the common strike differential less the net initial cash difference. The balance is the potential profit.

At expiration, the maximum cash gain is at the middle strike price for the underlying stock.

Possible Workout Against Key Measurements

The following is a summary of possible workout against key measurements on a package of three stocks to be detailed below:

	Debit Spd. (DS)	Cdt. Spd. (CS)	Option Capital (OC)	Comm. Strike Diff. (CSD)	Pot. Prof. (PP)	Prof. Lvge. (PL)
UPJ	$325	$200	$125	$500	$375	300%
XRX	$537	$237	$300	$1,000	$700	233%
EK	$463	$219	$244	$1,000	$756	310%

UPJOHN (UPJ)
2/24/75

Stock price=34⅞

Option prices: UPJ April 40=1¾
UPJ April 35=3¾
UPJ April 30=7

Option Strategy

Buy 1 UPJ April 40 at 1¾
Sell 2 UPJ April 35 at 3¾
Buy 1 UPJ April 30 at 7

(1) Buy 1 UPJ April 30 at 7
Sell 1 UPJ April 35 at 3¾
_____

Debit spread   3¼

(2) Sell 1 UPJ April 35 at 3¾
Buy 1 UPJ April 40 at 1¾
_____

Credit spread   2

Option Worksheet

(1) Debit Spread=3¼
(2) Credit Spread=2
(3) Option Capital (OC)=1¼

(4) Common Strike Differential (CSD)=5

(5) Profit Potential (PP)=CSD−OC=$375

(6) Profit Leverage (PL)= $\dfrac{PP}{OC}$=300%

XEROX (XRX)
2/24/75

Stock price=78⅝
Option prices: XRX April 90=2⅜
                      XRX April 80=5⅜
                      XRX April 70=10¾

Option Strategy
     Buy 1 XRX April 90 at 2⅜
     Sell 2 XRX April 80 at 5⅜
     Buy 1 XRX April 70 at 10¾

  (1) Buy 1 XRX April 70 at 10¾
      Sell 1 XRX April 80 at   5⅜
                     ―――――――――

               Debit spread   5⅜
  (2) Sell 1 XRX April 80 at 5⅜
      Buy 1 XRX April 90 at 2⅜

                     ―――――――――

              Credit spread 3

Option Worksheet
  (1) Debit Spread=5⅜
  (2) Credit Spread=2⅜
  (3) Option Capital (OC)=5⅜−2⅜=3
  (4) Common Strike Differential (CSD)=10
  (5) Profit Potential (PP)=CSD−OC=$700

  (6) Profit Leverage (PL)= $\dfrac{PP}{OC}$=233%

178

EASTMAN KODAK (EK)
2/24/75

Stock price = 86⅛

Option prices: EK April 100 = 1 11/16

EK April 90 = 3⅞

EK April 80 = 8½

Option Strategy

Buy 1 EK April 80 at 8½

Sell 1 EK April 90 at 3⅞

Debit Spread 4⅝

Sell 1 EK April 90 at   3⅞

Buy 1 EK April 100 at 1 11/16

Credit Spread 2 3/16

Option Worksheet

(1) Debit Spread = 4⅝

(2) Credit Spread = 2 3/16

(3) Option Capital (OC) = 2 7/16

(4) Common Strike Differential (CSD) = 10

(5) Profit Potential (PP) = CSD − OC = \$756

(6) Profit Leverage (PL) = $\dfrac{PP}{OC}$ = 310%

Portfolio Strategy

The initial phase of a "spread" portfolio for a pilot option money management program is suggested on a small scale, as follows:

15 "spreads" each on McDonald, Polaroid, and Disney as outlined above.

179

15 "sandwichs" each for Upjohn, Xerox, and Eastman
    Kodak as outlined above.

Portfolio Investment and Projected Returns
    The profit potential projected above, though not large
in amount, is extraordinarily high in terms of the gain per
dollar of cash investment, particularly with sandwich
spreads.
    The following is a summary of portfolio investment and
its possible returns (see Option Worksheets above):

Portfolio Options	No. of options	Unit price	Option Capital	Potential Profit	Profit Lvge
McDonald	15	× $350	$5,250	$4,515	86%
Polaroid	15	× $163	$2,445	$2,616	107%
Disney	15	× $413	$6,195	$2,602	42%
Upjohn	15	× $125	$1,875	$5,625	300%
Xerox	15	× $300	$4,500	$10,485	233%
Eastman Kodak	15	× $244	$3,660	$11,346	310%
			$23,925	$37,189	

    The potential profit leverage amounts to 155 percent
based on a profit of $37,189 on an option capital of $23,925.

DIAGONAL SPREADS

Combining Different Strikes and Different Expirations
    Basically, a diagonal spread is a "combination" spread
involving "long" and "short" positions of *both* different
striking prices *and* different maturity months.
    Whereas horizontal spreads and vertical spreads consist

of simultaneously buying and selling options on the same stock, with different striking prices *or* different expiration months, diagonal spreads involve such buying and selling with different striking prices *and* different expiration months.

Another Multiple Option Structure

Both diagonal spreads and sandwich spreads are forms of multiple option structures.

Whereas the sandwich spread, also known as a "butterfly," consists of the sale of two intermediate options and the purchase of two options with striking prices at equal distance from the "short" options in the ratio of 1:2:1, diagonal spreads combine simultaneous "long" and "short" positions combining different striking prices and different expiration months.

CHAPTER XV

OPTION PORTFOLIO STRATEGIES

Broad Option Strategy

Different market environments call for different option strategies, strategies that will also be determined by the overall objectives of the investor, whether individual or institutional.

Ratio Writing Strategy

If, with the market at a relatively high level, a cautious approach appears to be called for, stress should be on downside protection for the preservation of capital. A hedged option strategy called "ratio writing," if well structured, may provide a broad profit zone without compromising downside protection.

"Spreading" Strategy

Another comparatively new option strategy called "spreading" has rapidly gained in applications as a result of recently changed margin rules for spreads. The upshot of the new margin rules is that "spreading" has become a small-capital-expenditure investment medium, as the "long" option is deemed adequate to cover the "short" option.

Covered Writing Strategy

Despite the rising importance of "spreading" and "ratio

writing," covered writing remains the dominating factor in the mushrooming world of option strategies for the dual purposes of capital preservation and capital enhancement.

"Up," "Flat," or "Down" Market

In periods of market uncertainties, the built-in advantages enjoyed by covered option writers versus long common stock holders or call buyers are obvious. In an up market, the covered writer earns the premium and possibly favorable strike price differentials. In a flat market, the writer earns the option premium. In a down market, the writer may profit if the decline is less than the premium received.

The writer loses only when the decline is more than the premium received.

"Prototype" Portfolio

This chapter is designed to illustrate broad option strategies for an option-oriented portfolio of modest amounts, say, between $20,000 and $25,000, through the use of a "prototype" portfolio based on June 17, 1975, closing prices.

In other words, what are the possible approaches for option-bound investors who seek a small, diversified option portfolio for maximum profit potential and minimum risk exposure?

For such investors we use the prototype portfolio below for illustrative purposes. The word "illustrative" cannot be emphasized too strongly here since option suggestions are valid only at the time of making them, in view of literally minute-to-minute changes in the listed option market. Nor is this prototype portfolio intended to reflect the proportional balance of the components, in terms of invested funds, among the three principal categories of option

183

strategies: (1) Spreading, (2) Ratio Writing, and (3) Covered Writing.

This is because the values of particular options chosen for particular option strategies as of, say, June 17, 1975 (being the valuation date of this particular *sample* portfolio), would remain valid only for a limited time.

Portfolio Segments

Keeping the above in perspective, let us review the three segments of this prototype portfolio:

(A) "Spreading" Segment
(B) "Ratio Writing" Segment
(C) "Covered Writing" Segment

(A) "Spreading" Segment

1. "Special Situation" Spread: Bull "Perpendicular" on Eastman Kodak
   Cost: $525 per spread
   Reason: Possible 73.8-percent return in 18 weeks
   Size: 5 spreads, to cost $2,625

2. Bull "Vertical" on Xerox
   Cost: $213 per spread
   Reason: The long call potentially worth 10 points more than the short call
   Size: 5 spreads, to cost $1,065

3. Bull "Vertical" on Deere
   Cost: $200 per spread
   Reason: Narrow spread premium
   Size: 5 spreads, to cost $1,000

4. Bull "Horizontal" on IBM

Cost: $675 per spread
Reason: Possible widening of spread premium
Size: 2 spreads, to cost $1,350

(B) "Ratio Writing" Segment
1. 2-to-1 "ratio" write on Mesa Petroleum
   Cost: $1,875 per write
   Reason: Possible 28-percent return in 18 weeks if MSA remained unchanged at expiration
   Size: 1 "ratio" write, to cost $1,875

2. 2-to-1 "ratio" write on Pfizer
   Cost: $2,688 per write
   Reason: Fairly broad profit zone
   Size: 1 "write," to cost $2,688

3. 3-to-1 "ratio" write on Skyline
   Cost: $2,906 per write
   Reason: Broad profit zone
   Size: 1 "write," to cost $2,906.

4. 3-to-1 "ratio" write on Syntex
   Cost: $2,013 per write
   Reason: Broad profit zone
   Size: 1 "write," to cost $2,013.

(C) "Covered Writing" Segment
1. "Leveraged covered" write on Merrill Lynch
   Cost: $1,125 per "write"
   Reason: 28.6-percent downside protection; possible 34-percent return in less than 8 months if MER remained unchanged at expiration
   Size: 1 "write," to cost $1,125

185

2. Leveraged "covered" write on G. D. Searle
   Cost: $1,263 per "write"
   Reason: 32.7-percent downside protection; possible
   51.6-percent return in less than 9 months if SRL
   remained unchanged at expiration
   Size: 1 "write," to cost $1,263

3. "Covered" write on Disney
   Cost: $3,963 per "write"
   Reason: 19.6-percent downside protection; possible
   26.3-percent in 18 weeks if DIS were called
   Size: 1 "write," to cost $3,963

4. "Covered" write on Alcoa
   Cost: $3,863 per "write"
   Reason: 13.9-percent downside protection; 19.1-
   percent return in less than 9 months if AA were call-
   ed
   Size: 1 "write," to cost $3,863

Portfolio Cost Composition

The above portfolio would have composition and cost
structure as follows:

(A) "Spreading" Segment

	Cost
5 EK spreads	$2,625
5 XRX spreads	1,065
5 DE spreads	1,000
2 IBM spreads	1,350
	$6,040

186

(B) *"Ratio Writing" Segment*

1 MSA 2-to-1 write	$1,875
1 PFE 2-to-1 write	2,688
1 SKY 3-to-1 write	2,906
1 SYN 3-to-1 write	2,013
	9,482

(C) *"Covered Writing" Segment*

1 MER 1-to-1 leveraged write	$1,125
1 SRL 1-to-1 leveraged write	$1,263
1 DIS 1-to-1 write	$3,963
1 AA 1-to-1 write	$3,863
	$10,214

Total Portfolio Cost $25,736

ANATOMY OF "PROTOTYPE" PORTFOLIO

Following is an anatomy of the prototype portfolio.

(A). *"Spreading" Segment*

1. Special Situation Spread: Bull Perpendicular Spread

This is a low-cost special situation spread where you could possibly end with a 73.8-percent return in 18 weeks even with the underlying stock doing nothing during that intermediate-term option period.

It is based on a perpendicular spread on Eastman Kodak (NYSE-99⅛-EK) structured below:

```
Buy EK October 90 at    13¾
Sell EK October 100 at   8½
                        ─────
Cash layout              5¼
```

Also known as "vertical" or "money" spread, a perpendicular spread is an option technique that involves simultaneous long and short positions on the same stock having different strike prices but the same expiration month.

In bull "perpendiculars" you buy the low-strike option and sell (short) the high-strike option.

In our bull "horizontal" spreading on EK, you would need only $525 in cash layout to control a $99-plus stock for 18 weeks.

If EK remained unchanged at 99⅛ at October expiration, returns would be 73.8% over the 18-week time span.

With EK as a bull "perpendicular," the stock's expected upside move would considerably widen the premium spread from the current 5¼ points.

Every five-point move, or about 5 percent on a $99-value underlying stock, would probably magnify into a move of more than 20 percent, or more than three points in a 13¾-value option.

Meanwhile, the option premium would widen by about one point, or 20 percent or so, from the present 5¼ to 6¼.

2. *Bull Perpendicular Spread on Xerox*

For Xerox (NYSE-67¾-XRX) bulls, a low-cost

bull spread on XRX may be construed as follows:

Buy XRX October 80 at	3¾
Sell XRX October 90 at	1⅝
Cash layout	2⅛

With a 2⅛-point cash layout, a spreader can
own a XRX October 80 that potentially could
be worth ten points more than XRX 90.

3. Bull Perpendicular Spread on Deere

The following bull perpendicular spread appears attractive on Deere (NYSE-39½-DE):

Buy DE October 40 at	4
Sell DE October 45 at	2
Cash outlay	2

The maximum profit potential for this bull
spread is obtainable with DE moving up to 45.

4. Horizontal Spread on IBM

An attractive horizontal spread on IBM
(NYSE-203½) can be structured by the sale of
an intermediate-term option to reduce the cost
of a more-distant-term option that is believed
to be undervalued:

Buy IBM January 200 at	28
Sell IBM October 200 at	21¼
Cash outlay	6¾

Also known as a "calendar" or "time" spread, a horizontal spread is an option technique that involves buying and selling options having the same strike price but different expiration months. In bull "horizontals," you long the far-term expiration and sell (short) the near-term expiration.

Historically, the premium differential between an intermediate-term IBM option and a far-term IBM option with three months separating them, is wider than the spread premium of 6¾ indicated here.

The spreader's profit is predicated upon a possible widening of the spread premium.

(B) "Ratio Writing" Segment

1. 2-to-1 Ratio Write on Mesa Petroleum

Since well-structured partially hedged writing provides a broad "profit band" without compromising downside protection, the following two-against-one ratio writes appear attractive.

One involves Mesa (NYSE-24-MSA) with the following hedged construction.:

Buy MSA at 24
Sell 2 MSA October 25 calls at 2⅝ each
Downside Parameter 18¾
Upside Parameter   28⅛
Profit Zone   9⅜ points (between 28⅛
                              and 18¾)

A profit zone of 12½ points is thus established, within which the partial hedger will remain profitable.

2. *2-to-1 Ratio Write on Pfizer*

Pfizer (NYSE-30⅞-PFE) is another interesting partially hedged writing situation where you can construct a fairly broad profit zone between the upside and downside breakeven points within which PFE will remain profitable.

A 2-to-1 ratio write on PFE can be structured as follows:

Buy 100 PFE at	30⅞
Sell 2 October 35 calls at 2 each	
Downside Parameter	26⅞
Upside Parameter	43⅛
Profit zone	16¼ points

3. *3-to-1 Ratio Write on Skyline*

More aggressive hedgers may wish to go for a ratio of three to one.

An attractive 3-to-1 write involves selling August 25 calls at 1⅜ per call against 100 shares of Skyline (NYSE-21-SKY), as follows:

Buy 100 SKY at	21
Sell 3 SKY August 25 calls at 1⅜ each	
Downside Parameter	16⅞
Upside Parameter	29 1/16
Profit Zone	12 3/16 points

191

If SKY stayed unchanged at expiration, the 3-to-1 hedger would realize 24.4 percent in just five weeks.

4. 3-to-1 Ratio Write on Syntex

Syntex (NYSE-38⅛-SYN) is also promising as a 3-to-1 ratio write involving the sale of three SYN January 40 calls at 6 per call against 100 shares of SYN.

The partially hedged write is indicated by the following construction:

Buy 100 SYN at	38⅛
Sell 3 SYN January 40 calls at 6 each	
Downside Parameter	20⅛
Upside Parameter	49⅞
Profit Zone	29 5/16 points

If SYN remained unchanged at expiration, the ratio writer would gain 89.4 percent in less than eight months.

(C) "Covered Writing" Segment

Two situations appear particularly attractive for leveraged (margined) covered writing.

One would involve G. D. Searle (NYSE-18¾-SRL), a newcomer to the Amex, whose February 15 option provides a low-cost writing opportunity for very good returns.

The other one would involve Merrill Lynch (NYSE-15¾-MER), which continues to offer one of the most interesting writing possibilities.

1. "Leveraged Covered" Write on Merrill Lynch

Due to its predominantly retail business, MER has emerged competitively stronger and is likely to report higher-than-expected June quarter earnings.

A margined covered write on MER would involve purchasing 100 shares at 15¾ (margined at $787.50) and selling a January 15 call at 3⅜, as follows:

Buy 100 MER at	15¾
50% Margin at	7⅞
Sell MER January 15 at	3⅜
Cash Outlay	4½

Thus the option premium reduces cash outlays to $450 and protects the stock down to 12⅜ (27.3 percent).

2. "Leveraged Covered" Write on Searle

A leveraged covered writing structure is suggested on G. D. Searle as follows:

Buy 100 SRL at	18¾
50 percent Margin at	9⅜
Sell SRL February 15 at	6⅛
Cash outlay	3¼

Thus, the option premium from the sale of the "deep in the money" February 15 call reduces cash requirement to $3.25 and, simultaneously, protects the stock down to 12⅝ (32.7 percent).

The likely high return is due to the low cash outlay of this leveraged covered writing structure as well as by SRL's "deep in the money" option.

It is worthy of note here that option-oriented investors should be alert to new option opportunities. It would be worth watching first-hour trading for possible aberrations because frequently new options tend to be very underpriced or overpriced.

3. Covered Write on Disney

The following two covered option writing situations offer the potential for attractive returns if the underlying stock were called away (all on a cash basis).

One situation involves writing an October 50 option at 7¾ on Disney (NYSE-47⅝-DIS) against 100 shares of DIS, with the option premium reducing the covered writer's cash outlay to 39⅞, as follows:

Buy 100 DIS at	47⅝
Sell DIS October 50 at	7¾
Cash outlay	39⅞

The reduced investment at 39⅝ also provides the downside protection (16.4 percent).

If DIS were called away at 50, the gain to the covered writer would total $1,037.50, including $775 from option premium and 2⅝ from appreciation to the called-away price, indicating a return of 26.2 percent in 18 weeks.

4. *Covered Write on Alcoa*

Another covered writing situation involves issuing a January 45 option at 5⅜ on Alcoa (NYSE-44-AA) against 100 shares of stock, as follows:

Buy 100 AA at	44
Sell AA January 45 at	5⅜
Cash outlay	38⅝

The reduced cash outlay of 38⅝ also provides the downside protection (12.2 percent).

If the underlying security were called away at 45, the gain to the covered writer would total $738, including 5⅜ from the option premium, one point from appreciation to the called-away price, and $100.50 from dividends, indicating a return of 19.1 percent in less than eight months.

Portfolio Methods

While the prototype portfolio is only valid at the time of construction, what is "timeless" are the methods of composing an option portfolio through the use of different option media and strategies.

Also timeless are the methods of achieving portfolio leverage through ratio writing and spreading techniques, to maximize investment results, as well as those methods designed to achieve the dual objectives of capital preservation and capital enhancement, particularly during periods of market uncertainties.

CHAPTER XVI

MARGIN REQUIREMENTS

Margin's Two Edges

Margin is a term used at the marketplace to indicate borrowing from a broker for achieving leverage. In return, a broker needs protection for his lending through actual cash or collateral deposited by the borrowing investor.

Leveraged investment with borrowed money serves to magnify gains if such investment is based on sound and correct judgment. Conversely, leverage can work against an investor and magnify his losses if his investment decisions should prove to be wrong. Investors should be fully aware of the perils of "margin calls," which are very real, as well as of the possibilities of involuntary liquidation of their accounts, especially in periods of severe market declines such as we witnessed in 1973 and 1974.

Three Sets of Margin Requirements

For any given margin security, an investor is required to comply with the highest of the three sets of margin requirements established, respectively, by the Federal Reserve Board via Regulation T, the New York Stock Exchange, and the "house" (a New York Stock Exchange member firm).

Margin and Credit Relationships

Since The Options Clearing Corporation (OCC) acts as

197

the central clearing house for listed options, it requires each clearing member firm either to deposit the underlying stock or to maintain margin with the OCC in any one or any combination of the three specified types of margin:

1. cash;
2. U.S. Treasury Bills; and
3. a letter of credit issued by a commercial bank rated acceptable by OCC.

In return, clearing member firms are required to comply with the credit between a member firm and its customers.

Regulation T

Regulation T of the Federal Reserve Board governs, among other things, the amount of credit (if any) that initially may be extended by a broker to his customer.

For purposes of Regulation T, listed options have no loan value. Full payment for purchase of such options must be made within the required time limit, although such options may be purchased either in a special cash account or in a margin account.

Brokerage firms are also required to comply with the margin requirements of the exchanges of which they are members. Amex margin requirements, with respect to listed options, are substantially similar to those of the New York Stock Exchange.

Moreover, brokerage firms may impose "house" rules that are never less, but rather more, strict than those of Regulation T and the exchanges.

Margin-Account-Only Transactions

Certain transactions must take place in margin accounts.

Generally, covered writing transactions may be effected in a margin account or in a special cash account, but only if the underlying security is held in the account.

Uncovered writing transactions and option spread transactions in listed options must take place in a margin account.

A call option may be exercised in a special cash account if full cash payment is made promptly.

Where a call is held in a margin account and is exercised, the initial margin requirement of Regulation T applies to the purchase price of the stock.

However, if a call is exercised in a margin account and the underlying stock is sold on the same day, no additional margin is required under Regulation T if the proceeds from the sale exceed the exercise price of the call.

Initial Margin Requirement

Since January 1974 the Federal Reserve Board has established the initial margin requirement at 50 percent for purchase long or sale short of equity securities.

Both the New York Stock Exchange and the Amex require an initial margin minimum of $2,000 that applies to all new securities transactions and commitments. Thereafter the maintenance margin provisions apply.

The $2,000 initial margin (also called "minimum account equity") rule has exceptions. For one thing, if a proposed purchase will cost less than $2,000, the customer need not deposit more than the actual purchase price for the transaction.

For another, with regard to certain "speculative" transactions, including short sales or uncovered option transactions, an equity of $2,000 is required after such transactions.

199

Maintenance Margin

Under New York Stock Exchange maintenance margin provisions, generally an account is required to maintain a minimum 25-percent equity in the account. Defined as the customer's ownership interest in the account, equity is arrived at by subtracting his debit balance from the present market value of the securities in the account. "Margin calls" would be in order if securities value declines to this minimum maintenance level.

The New York Stock Exchange and Amex have established similar minimum maintenance margin requirements as follows:

Margins for Covered Option Transactions

No margin is required for sale of call options against "long" position. The "long" position can be either "long" stock in the account and properly margined, or the broker is in possession of an escrow receipt or an option-guarantee letter issued by a bank or trust company approved by OCC.

Margins for Uncovered Option Transactions

For sale of call options without "long" stock, the requirement is 30 percent of the current market value of the underlying security

    (a) *plus* 100 percent of any excess of the current market value of the underlying security over the aggregate exercise price of the call (in the money), or

    (b) *minus* 100 percent of any excess of the aggregate exercise price of the call over the current market value of the underlying security (out of the money), with a minimum requirement of $250 per option contract.

In other words—(a) if the stock is selling higher than the striking price (in the money), the margin requirement is 30 percent of the market price of the stock *plus* the differential between the market price and the striking price; (b) if the stock is selling below the striking price (out of the money), the margin requirement is 30 percent of the market price of the stock, *minus* the differential between market price and striking price.

Illustration #1. "Short" Uncovered Option with Market Price Same as Striking Price

Assuming that an investor wrote one uncovered Weyerhaeuser (WY) October 40 for 3½ when WY common stock was at 40 (based on June 24, 1975, closing prices), the maintenance margin would be:

30% of WY ($4,000 × .30) . . . $1,200
Plus In the money 0
Minus Out of the money 0

Maintenance Margin
Requirement $1,200

The option premium of $350 received from sale of the uncovered WY October 40 option may be used to satisfy part of the maintenance margin requirement. If, however, the equity in the account was less than $2,000 at the time of the transaction, the initial margin requirement of $2,000 must be satisfied.

Illustration #2. "Short" Uncovered Option with Market Price Above Striking Price

If, thereafter, WY went up to $50, the maintenance margin requirement would be:

30% of WY ($5,000 × .30) . . .$1,500
Plus In the money ($5,000-$4,000) $1,000

Maintenance Margin
Requirement $2,500

Illustration #3. "Short" Uncovered Option with Market Price Below Striking Price

If WY, thereafter, went down to $35, the maintenance margin requirement would be:

30% of WY ($3,500 x .30) . . .$1,050
Less Out of the money ($4,000–$3,500) 500

Maintenance Margin Requirement $550

Sale of Put Options

No margin is required on sale of a put option against "short" stock.

On sale of a put option without "short" stock, the minimum maintenance requirement is 25 percent of the market price of the underlying stock

(a) *plus* the differential between the market price and the striking price, if the market price is lower than the striking price; or

(b) *minus* the differential between the market price and the striking price, if the market price is higher than the striking price.

SPREAD MARGINS

Following is a summary of margin requirements on those spreads where a "long" call may margin a "short" call.

Margins on "Bull Horizontal" Spreads

"Bull horizontal" spreads are those where the "long" option expires no earlier than the "short" option.

The maintenance margin requirement on such spreads is the *lesser* of

(a) the margin required against the "short" option if treated as uncovered, with a $250 minimum per option contract, or

(b) the excess, if any, of the aggregate exercise price of the "long" option over the aggregate exercise price of the "short" option.

Illustration #4. "Long" Far Expiration, "Short" Near Expiration at Same Striking Price

Assume an investor wrote one Honeywell (HON) October 40 for 5¼ and, at the same time, bought one HON January 40 for 7 when HON common was at $40 (based on June 25, 1975, closing prices).

This "bull horizontal" spread would qualify for spread margin treatment because the "long" position would expire no earlier than the "short" position.

The maintenance margin requirement would be the lesser of:

30% of HON ($4,000 × .30) $1,200
Plus In the money   0
Minus Out of the money   0

$1,200

or

Differential between striking prices
($4,000−$4,000) 0
Maintenance Margin Requirement 0

No maintenance margin is required on the "short" position because the "long" position more than covers the "short" position:

"Long" position (January 40) at 7
"Short" position (October 40) at 5¼

1¾

In addition to the $525 from writing HON October 40, which is applicable toward the $700 purchase price of the "long" position, an additional $175 is required to satisfy the requirement that a "long" option must be paid for in full. In addition, the initial margin requirement must also be met if the equity in the account is less than $2,000 at the time of the transaction.

Margins On "Bear Horizontal" Spreads

"Bear horizontal" spreads are those where the "long" option expires earlier than the "short" option. In other words, you "long" the near expiration and "short" the far expiration on the same stock, with the two options having the same striking price.

Spread margins are not applicable to "bear horizontal" spreads. Such margins apply only to those spreads where the number of "long" options equals or exceeds the number of "short" options.

"Uncovered short" options must be margined as uncovered call options.

> *Illustration #5. "Long" Near Expiration, "Short" Far Expiration at Same Striking Price*
>
> Assuming that an investor wrote a Boeing (BA) October 30 for 4⅜ and, at the same time, bought a BA July 30 for 3½ when BA common was at 31⅛ (based on June 25, 1975, closing prices), this "bear horizontal" spread would not qualify for spread margins because the "long" position expires prior to the "short" position.
>
> In this case, the "short" position must be margined as an "uncovered short" and the "long" position must be paid in full.

Margins on "Vertical" Spreads

"Vertical" spreads involve buying and selling (shorting) options on the same stock having the same expiration month but different striking prices.

Spread margins are applicable to "verticals" where

"long" options have the *same* expiration month as "short" options.

Illustration #6. *"In the Money" Vertical Spread*

Assuming that an investor wrote a General Motors (GM) October 35 for 11⅜ and, at the same time, bought a GM October 40 for 7½ when GM common was at 46 (based on June 25 closing prices), the maintenance margin requirement would be the lesser of

30% of GM ($4,600 × .30)	$1,380
Plus In the money ($4,600–$3,500)	$1,100
	$2,480

or

Differential between striking prices	
($4,000 – $3,500)	$500
Maintenance Margin Requirement .	$500

As always, the minimum account equity of $2,000 must be met if the equity in the account is below that amount at the time of the transaction.

The difference between the premium received ($1,138) from the "short" position and the premium paid ($750) for the "long" position, amounting to $388, would be applicable toward meeting the initial margin requirement.

Illustration #7. *"Out of the Money" Vertical Spread*

If GM common later declined to

$30, the maintenance margin requirement would be the lesser of

30% of GM ($3,000 × .30) $900
Less Out of the money
($3,500−$3,000) $500

$400

or

Differential between striking prices
($4,000−$3,500) $500
Maintenance Margin Requirement $400

CHAPTER XVII

BASIC TAX FACTORS

Different Tax Values

Different tax treatments governing buying and selling options create different values.

For option sellers (writers), for instance, premiums received from selling (writing) options (whether put or call), are deferred assets until the options either expire or are exercised.

The short call (i.e., written) gain or loss is ordinary. Ordinary loss is deductible without limit from ordinary gain.

For the option buyers, premiums paid for options are treated as nondeductible capital expenditures.

The gain or loss from long call (i.e., bought) is taxed as a capital item, long or short, depending on the time period held.

Tax-Dictated Option Approaches

For investors, especially those with high income or capital losses, tax considerations may dictate different approaches.

If an investor sold a call and closed out his option position at a loss, this would be a deduction from ordinary income.

If, however, at the same time as he sold the call, he

purchased another call in the same security with either a different striking price or a different expiration date, and if he succeeded in closing out the second option at a profit, this profit would be taxed as a capital gain that could be used to offset his already sustained capital losses on a dollar-to-dollar basis.

The following is a summary of basic tax factors on options for individual and corporate nondealer taxpayers.

BASIC TAX FACTORS FOR SELLERS (WRITERS)

1. Option Sale
The premium received from sale of an option (whether call or put) is a deferred asset until the option either expires or is exercised.

2. If Option Is Not Exercised
If the option is not exercised, the premium money becomes ordinary income to the seller.

3. If Option Is Exercised

(A) Call Option
If a call option is exercised, the premium received from the sale of the option is deemed to have increased the sale price of the underlying stock. The result is treated as a capital gain or loss, depending upon the holding period of the stock only.

The factor determining short-term or long-term tax treatment is not the length of time involved on the call option, but the holding period of the underlying stock.

(B) Put Option

If a put option is exercised, the premium received from the sale of the option is deemed to have reduced the purchase price of the underlying stock and, therefore, qualifies for capital gains treatment.

The capital gains holding period begins when the stock is acquired, not when the original put transaction is entered into.

4. Closing a Writing (Selling) Position:

When an option writer closes a writing position, the difference between the premium initially received for writing the option and the amount paid later for buying the option is treated as ordinary income or loss.

Tax-Shaping Option Transactions

Options provide a means of facilitating tax planning for an option writer through judicious selection of the form of option transaction.

Tax Shelter Strategies

For substantial investors, options can be used as one of the most interesting tax shelters available to-day.

Certain substantial investors may be more interested in converting ordinary income to capital gains (long- or short-term) than in potential market gains with their inherent risks.

Different tax shelter methods are available to achieve the above objectives. Among option-oriented tax shelter strategies is the so-called "closing purchase" technique.

"Closing Purchase" Technique

A "closing purchase" transaction is one involving purchase of an offsetting option to close out an existing option obligation already written.

Assume you bought 1,000 shares of XYZ at 25 and sold ten July 25 calls against the stock for a total premium of $4,000 ($400 per call).

If XYZ is now 45 after a six-month-plus holding period, you could, before an unwelcome exercise of your sold options before their expiration date, effect a "closing purchase" transaction whereby you would "close" out the outstanding options by buying them back at a cost of, say, $20,000, and, at the same time, sell 1,000 shares of XYZ at 45, to have a long-term profit of $25,000 ($45,000 as stock-sale price less $20,000 as cost of the new offsetting options bought).

How To Create Ordinary Loss with an Offsetting Option

From the above "closing-purchase" option transaction, you would create an ordinary loss of $16,000 ($20,000 as cost of "closing purchase" less the original option premium of $4,000 received). This ordinary loss would be fully deductible from your ordinary income.

If Stock Remains Same or Went Lower

What would happen to you if XYZ remained only slightly above the exercise price at the end of the option period. In that event, you would allow the option to be exercised. In effect, you would sell the stock at the exercise price plus premium.

If the stock should go measurably below the exercise price, the buyer would let the option expire. While your underlying stock would be trading at a measurable loss, the premium you had received from the sold option would serve somewhat to offset the loss. The premium would be subject to ordinary income tax treatment.

Converting Short-Term To Long-Term Gain

For an option seller writing a six-months-ten-day call option for, say, $500 against 100 shares of XYZ that he had bought at a lower price (for example, 60), he could use the call option as a means of converting short-term gains to long-term gains if the underlying stock has a substantial rise to a higher price, say of 90, in the following way.

How To Create Ordinary Loss with Offsetting Stock

If the stock now has been held for more than six months and one day, he may sell the stock at 90, taking a long-term profit of $3,000. Simultaneously, he may buy an additional 100 shares of the stock at 90. (Wash sale rules apply only to loss-taking but not to profit-taking).

When the original call option sold with a strike price of $60 were subsequently exercised against him, he delivers the new 100 shares recently bought at 90, to create a short term loss of $3,000 less the call premium of $500 received.

This transaction will, in effect, have converted about $2,500 ($3,000 less premium of $500), taxwise, from a short-term gain to a long-term gain, assuming that he has already accumulated that much short-term gain.

Modified Strategy

A modified form of the above option tax shelter technique is also designed to use options as a means of carrying a short-term stock (if it is profitable) into a long-term stock.

If you have such a profitable stock held for three

months, you may sell a three-month call option against that stock.

In this way, you "lock in" your gain while waiting out the six-month-and-one-day long-term holding period.

If the stock were called before the long-term six-month holding, you could repeat the previously described technique by purchasing new stock to deliver against the call. This would create a short-term loss. You would hold the older stock until it would be six months and one day old.

BASIC TAX FACTORS FOR OPTION BUYERS

The same tax considerations applicable to call options also apply to put options.

1. Option Purchase

Premiums paid for options purchased are treated as nondeductible capital expenditures.

2. If Option Is Not Exercised

If the buyer lets a call option or put option expire without exercising it, he has a long-term or short-term capital loss, depending on the length of time the option has been held.

3. If Option Is Exercised
(A) Call Option

If a call option is exercised, the premium is added to the price of the called stock to determine cost.

(B) Put Option

If a put option holder exercises his option,

the premium paid for the option is deemed, for tax purposes, to have reduced the sale price of the stock.

Put option holders enjoy one outstanding advantage over short sellers.

For short sellers, profits made on a short sale are always treated as short-term for tax purposes, regardless of how long the short seller has held the position.

On the other hand, profits made from a put option are treated as a long-term capital gain if a put option buyer has held the option for six months and ten days—a normal time unit with options—and he sells the actual put paper at the end of six months and one day.

4. Option Sale in Closing Transaction
Sale of an option in a closing transaction is treated either as a long-term or short-term capital gain or loss depending on the holding period of the option.

Tax Strategies for Option Buyers
The most important tax advantage for option buyers is the distinct tax benefits that put option buyers enjoy over short sellers.

While this advantage was mentioned previously, it deserves special elaboration here.

Comparative Tax-Treatment Methods
While profits made from a short position cannot, in any

circumstances, result in a long-term gain, a put option can be resold for a long-term gain or loss if it has been held for more than six months.

However, the short sale rule would apply if a put option is purchased to protect a short-term profit. The short sale rule would be operative here because the holding period of the stock is considered to have been interrupted. Thus, the ensuing gain upon the exercise of the put option would be deemed short-term even if the stock has been held for more than six months.

If the put option is allowed to expire, the new holding period of the stock starts with the expiration date of the put option.

Hedge-Identifying Status

The short sale rule does not apply only if the put option is identified as a hedge; that is, the put option is purchased simultaneously with the underlying stock.

Then, if the put option is allowed to expire or is used to sell the original stock underlying the put option, the holding period of the put option is considered, taxwise, to have started with the purchase date of the stock.

The short sale rule becomes operative only if the put option is resold separately or exercised to sell stock purchased at a different date. In that event, the holding period of the original stock would begin with the exercise or resale of the put option.

Other Applications for Option Buyers

Options can be used for a significant number of other tax-sheltering or tax-reducing applications.

Important among such applications are those used as

215

means of realizing a long-term gain whether on advance or decline of the underlying security.

To Realize Long-Term Gain on a Decline

Put options provide a means of realizing a long-term gain on stock decline.

Buying of a put option would give the buyer the dual advantages of predetermined risk (cost of the put option) and, at the same time, the potential for long-term capital gain.

Assume you buy a six-month-ten-day put option for, say, $800 on XYZ instead of "shorting" the stock.

If XYZ declined, as anticipated, at the end of the option period, you could sell the profitable put option as a capital asset at its then market value of, perhaps, $3,000, instead of exercising the put option. Your profit would be $3,000, less $800 as the cost of the put option, amounting to $2,200 that you could declare as a long-term capital gain.

Had you sold the stock short, your profits would be $3,000, but subject to short-term tax treatment.

To Realize Long-Term Gain on a Rise

The same technique can be used to realize a long-term gain on stock rise, through a call option, just as through a put option on stock decline.

Instead of exercising the call option, you could sell the option as a capital asset at its then market value, which would be subject to long-term capital gains treatment.

Had you exercised the option, the gain from the exercise would have to be held for an additional six months to qualify for long-term capital gains.

Tax Considerations for Straddles

Under Internal Revenue Service rules, the premium

from straddle options is divided unequally, with 45 percent of the money allocated to the put side and 55 percent to the call side.

Other allocations, however, such as one based on 50 percent for the call portion and 50 percent for the put portion, would also be acceptable to the Internal Revenue Service, so long as such allocations are made uniformly and consistently.

Either or Both Sides of Straddle Exercised

Once a straddle writer has made his premium allocation, normally 55 percent for the call option and 45 percent for the put option, any gain from any portion of the straddle that subsequently lapses is considered, taxwise, as a short-term capital gain, not straight income.

Also, the premium allocated to the unexercised portion will remain a short-term gain even if the straddle option is issued for more than six months.

If either or both sides of the straddle are exercised, which normally is rare, the put portion of the premium lowers the cost of the stock while the call portion of the premium raises it.

Summary

Since tax aspects of option transactions sometimes involve very complex areas, option-oriented investors would do well to consult their tax advisors in each instance.

All premiums received from the sale of a put or call are held in abeyance until the option expires or is exercised. In all cases where an option expires unexercised, the premium is considered as ordinary income in the year the option expires.

When a profitable call option is exercised, the premium is added to the selling price. On the other hand, when a profitable put is exercised, the premium is subtracted from the buying price.

Importance of Timing
Since put and call options affect the buyer's tax position at the time they are exercised or expire, it is extremely important for the option buyer to know when gains or losses should be declared for tax purposes.

Key to Tax Shelters
It is for sellers, or writers, of options that the best tax shelter opportunities open up.

The key to the situation is that the writer of an option at any time prior to receiving an exercise notice from his broker, can buy back the call he has previously written and identify the purchase as a closing transaction. Any profit or loss is ordinary income or loss.

Call options are likely to be exercised ahead of time until such time as the call sells for less than the spread between the exercise price and the market price. In that event the entire transaction would result in a small profit.

CHAPTER XVIII

OPTION WORKSHOP

Basic Option Worksheet

Since option writing is generally considered the most prudent form of option investing, we will use the basic option writing worksheet for illustrative purposes.

A basic option writing worksheet includes the following elements:

A. Basic data
B. "Buy stock" data
C. "Sell option" data
D. Possible consequences:
 (x) if stock moves above striking price, with option exercised;
 (y) if stock remains unchanged; and
 (z) if stock moves lower.

Basic Data

a. Date ....
b. Number of Calendar Days ....
c. Name of Stock ....
d. Number of Shares ....
e. Purchase Price ....
f. Option ....
g. Premium ....

219

    h. Dividend ....XD*...............
       Dividend ....XD ....
       Dividend ....XD ....
       Total Dividends ....

Buy Stock
    1. Cost of Stock Purchase ....
    2. (Plus) Commission on Stock Purchase ....
    3. Total Stock Cost ....

Sell Option
    4. Gross Premium Receipt ....
    5. (Minus) Commission on Option Sale ....
    6. Net Premium Receipt ....

Actual Cash Investment
    3. Total Stock Cost ....
    6. (Minus) Net Premium Receipt ....
    7. Actual Cash Investment ....

POSSIBLE CONSEQUENCES

The following are possible consequences:

(x) if stock moves above striking price, with option exercised;

(y) if stock remains unchanged; and

(z) if stock moves lower.

If Stock Moves Above Striking, with Option Exercised
    6. Net Premium Receipt ....
    8. (Plus) Dividends ....

*XD: Ex-dividend Date

9. (Plus or minus) Gain or Loss ....
2. (Minus) Commission on Stock Purchase ....
10. (Minus) Commission on Exercise ....
11. Net Return ....
12. Percent Gain (line 11÷line 7) ....
   for ———— days.
13. Annualized Gain* ————————%

If Stock Remains Unchanged
6. Net Premium Receipt ....
14. (Minus) Amount (if any) of Option in Money .....
8. (Plus) Dividends ....
2. (Minus) Commission on Stock Purchase ....
15. Net Return ....
16. Percent Gain (line 15÷line 7) ....
   for ———— days
13. Annualized Gain ————————%

If Stock Moves Lower
3. Total Stock Cost ....
6. (Minus) Net Premium Receipt ....
8. (Minus) Dividends ....
17. Investment Reduced to ....
18. Breakeven Point (line 17÷no. of shares) ....

Illustrative Transaction
Applying the above option worksheet formula to an il-
lustrative transaction on Philip Morris (NYSE-46-MO) on
March 19, 1975, that would involve buying 100 shares of
MO at 46 and selling one July 50 call at 3⅝, we had the
following:

*Multiply Percent Gain by 360 and divide by number of days.

a. Date   3/19/75
b. Number of Calendar Days   129
c. Name of Stock   Philip Morris
d. Number of Shares   100
e. Purchase Price   46
f. Option   July 50
g. Premium   3⅜
h. Dividend $0.225   XD 6/11/75
   Dividend ——————— XD ——————
   Dividend ——————— XD ——————
   Total Dividends $0.225

APPLYING WORKSHEET FORMULA

Buy Stock
   1. Cost of Stock Purchase $4,600.00
   2. (Plus) Commission on Stock Purchase $62.00
   3. Total Stock Cost $4,662.00

Sell Option
   4. Gross Premium Receipt $337.50
   5. (Minus) Commission on Option Sale $15.00
   6. Net Premium Receipt $322.50

Actual Cash Investment
   3. Total Stock Cost $4,662.00
   6. (Minus) Net Premium Receipt $322.50
   7. Actual Cash Investment $4,339.50

POSSIBLE CONSEQUENCES

If Stock Moves Above Striking, with Option Exercised
   6. Net Premium Receipt $322.50
   8. (Plus) Dividends $22.50

9. Gain or Loss $400.00
2. (Minus) Commission on Stock Purchase 62.00
10. (Minus) Commission on Exercise $65.00
11. Net Return $618.00
12. Percent Gain $(11 \div 7) = 14.2$
for 129 days
13. Annualized Gain 39.6%

If Stock Remains Unchanged

6. Net Premium Receipt $322.50
14. (Minus) Amount (if any) of Option in Money 0
8. (Plus) Dividends $22.50
2. (Minus) Commission on Stock Purchase $62.00
15. Net Return $283.00
16. Percent Gain $(15 \div 7) = 6.5$
13. Annualized Gain 18.1%

If Stock Moves Lower

3. Total Stock Cost $4,662.00
6. (Minus) Net Premium Receipt $322.50
8. (Minus) Dividends $22.50
17. Investment Reduced to $4,317.00
18. Breakeven Point $43.17

Do-It-Yourself Option Assessment

By application of the above option worksheet formulas, readers should be able to work out their own option sheets as a means of assessing the relative returns of varying option writing possibilities.

GLOSSARY OF OPTION TERMS

Annualized Return:
> The calculated hypothetical return, on an annualized basis, for an option purchaser or writer (seller) based on the conditions that might exist at the expiration of an option contract. Such return is the aggregate sum of proceeds from option premium, possible appreciation to expiration, and dividends. Such hypothetical return, however, rarely occurs.

Annualized Yield:
> Same as Annualized Return.

Arbitrage:
> An offsetting transaction, involving almost simultaneous purchases and sales of the same security, or substantiially identical securities, in different markets in order to profit from a price differential.

"At Market" Options:
> Options whose exercise (striking) price is equal to the current market value of the underlying security.

Bear Horizontal Spread:
> An option spread involving the purchase of the near-month expiration and the sale of the more-distant-month expiration.

Bear Straddle Writing:

Selling (writing) one call option against cash and one put option against a "long" position.

Bear Vertical Spread:

The reverse of a bull vertical spread—buying higher-strike option(s) and selling (shorting) lower-strike option(s).

Bull Horizontal Spread:

An option spread involving the purchase of the more-distant-month expiration and the sale of the near-month expiration.

Bull Straddle Writing:

Selling (writing) one call option against a long position and one put option against cash.

Bull Vertical Spread:

The reverse of a bear vertical spread—buying low-strike option and selling high-strike option. Bull "vertical" spread is sometimes called bull "perpendicular" or bull "money" spread.

Butterfly:

An option spread consisting of the sale of two intermediate options and the purchase of two options with striking prices of equal distance from the "short" options, in the ratio of 1:2:1. A "butterfly" is sometimes called "sandwich" spread.

Buy-Stop:

An option strategy whereby an uncovered option writer executes an order normally on the basis of the striking price plus option premium. The purpose of a "buy-stop" order is to limit an unknown loss.

Buying In:

Eliminating an option writer's obligation rising out of the prior sale of a call option through purchasing a similar call option and designating it a closing transaction.

CBOE:

The Chicago Board Options Exchange.

"Calendar" Spread:

A spread involving simultaneous buying and selling of options having the same striking price but different expiration months. A "calendar" spread is sometimes called "time" or "horizontal" spread.

Call Option:

An option contract giving the option buyer the right to buy 100 shares of a specific stock at a specific price for a specific period of time.

Clearing Member:

A member of a national securities exchange who has become a clearing member of the Options Clearing Corporation.

Closing Call:

The purchase by an option writer, normally uncovered, of a call option with the same expiration date and striking price as the previously sold one.

Closing Purchase Transaction:

A transaction in which an investor who has previously written (sold) an option intends to liquidate his pre-existing position as a writer. This liquidation is accomplished by "buying" in a closing purchase transaction an option having the same terms as the option previously written. Such a transaction has the effect of canceling an investor's pre-existing position as a writer, instead of resulting in the issuance of an option to the investor.

Closing Sale Transaction:

A transaction in which an investor who has previously purchased an option intends to liquidate his pre-existing position as a holder. This liquidation is accomplished by "selling" in a closing sale transaction an option having the same terms as the option previously bought. Such a transaction has the effect of liquidating the investor's pre-existing position as a holder of the option, instead of resulting in the investor's assuming the obligation of a writer.

Closing Transaction:

The purchase or sale of an option for the purpose of offsetting and canceling an existing open position resulting from a prior sale or purchase.

Continuous Auction Market:

One of the major ingredients of a listed options market, where a continuous auction market in standardized option contracts enables holders and writers of options to liquidate their positions as easily and as simply as other securities listed on major stock exchanges.

Conversion:

A process of converting one side of a straddle option contract into the other side, with the striking price remaining the same. Such conversion in the listed options market is different from the over-the-counter options market where conversion of a straddle option contract (composed of a put and a call) would result in either two puts or two calls.

Conversion Charge:

The cost of converting the put portion of a straddle option contract into a call. This cost normally is larger than the Reverse Charge that represents the cost of converting the call portion of a straddle option into a put. The smaller reverse charge is because no stock purchase is required.

Covered Writer:

A writer of an option who, so long as he remains a writer, owns the shares or other units of an underlying security covered by the option.

Covered Writing:

Selling (writing) an option contract involving a number of shares covered by an equal number of shares owned, and preparing to deliver these shares in the event that the option buyer calls for delivery through exercise of his option right.

"Deep in the Money" Option:

An option is said to be deep in the money when its price rises substantially above the intrinsic value.

228

Diagonal Spread:
> A spread involving simultaneous buying and selling options with different striking prices and different expiration months.

"Discount" Option:
> An option is said to have sold at discount when the premium plus the exercise (striking) price is less than the current market price of the underlying security.

Downside Parameter:
> The downside price level of the underlying security below which a ratio writer will incur a loss.

"Even" Spread:
> A spread is said to be "even" when the cost of the "long" option equals the cost of the "short" option.

Exercise Price:
> The price per unit at which the holder of an option may purchase the underlying security upon exercise. The exercise price is sometimes called the "striking price."

Expiration Date:
> The last day of an option period in which a listed call option may be exercised. Option holders should determine from their brokers the time limit for instructing the broker to exercise an option, so that the expiration deadline, when an exercise notice must be received at the Options Clearing Corporation, may be met.

Expiration Months:

> The series of expiration months currently in force include either the April-July-October-January series or the May-August-November-February series.

Far Option:

> That portion of a spread option whose expiration date arrives last.

Half Hedge:

> Writing (selling) two option contracts for each 100 shares of the underlying security owned.

Hedge Buying:

> Buying a call option contract and offsetting that purchase either through selling the underlying security short or selling (writing) a call option contract with the same exercise price but a different expiration date.

Hedge Writing:

> Writing (selling) a call option contract and offsetting that sale either through buying an equal number of shares in the underlying security or positioning an over-the-counter call option.

Horizontal Spread:

> A spread involving simultaneous buying and selling of options having the same striking price but different expiration months. A horizontal spread is sometimes called "time" or "calendar" spread.

In the Money:

> The exercise (striking) price of an option contract is be-

low the current market price of the underlying stock.

"In the Money" Option:
> An option whose exercise (striking) price is below the current market price of the underlying security.

Intrinsic Value:
> The difference between the market value of the underlying security and the exercise (striking) price of the option, but less than zero. Intrinsic value is sometimes called "tangible value."

Liquidity:
> The liquid ability of listed options to convert to and from cash, due to the existence of a secondary market for such options on a continuous basis.

Listed Call Option:
> A contract given for an agreed premium, entitling the buyer or holder, at his option, to buy on or before a fixed date, 100 shares of a specific, widely held, actively traded security at a predetermined price.

Maintenance Margin:
> The maintenance margin provisions of the New York Stock Exchange concerning the minimum equity level required of an account after meeting the initial margin requirements.

Margin:
> The amount of borrowing or credit that a broker is permitted to extend to his customers in option transactions.

Maximum Loss:

The calculated maximum exposure of an option buyer or writer (seller) when he enters into a buying or writing (selling) transaction.

Maximum Return:

The calculated maximum return for an option purchaser or writer (seller) based on the conditions that might exist at the expiration of an option contract. Such return is the aggregate sum of proceeds from option premium, possible appreciation to expiration, and dividends.

"Money" Spread:

A spread involving simultaneous buying and selling of options having the same expiration month but different striking prices. A "money" spread is sometimes called "vertical" or "perpendicular" spread.

Naked Writer:

An option writer who does not own the shares or other units of the underlying security covered by the option. A naked writer is also called uncovered writer.

Naked Writing:

Writing (selling) an option with the writer (seller) owning no shares or other units of the underlying security covered by the option.

Near Option:

That portion of a spread option whose expiration date arrives first.

Offsetting Call Option:

An option that an uncovered option writer may buy on the same underlying security to cover his "naked" option sale.

Open Position:

A position following (1) an option sale wherein the option has not expired or been exercised; or (2) an option purchase wherein the option has not been exercised or nullified by becoming worthless at expiration.

Opening Purchase Transaction:

A transaction in which an investor tends to become the holder of an option.

Opening Sale Transaction:

A transaction in which an investor intends to become the writer of an option.

Option:

Unless otherwise noted, options in this book pertain to listed call options that may be purchased or sold in transactions on one or more national securities exchanges.

Option Period:

The time period during which the option buyer must exercise or lose his right to buy according to the terms of the option contract.

Options Clearing Corporation:

The central options clearing agency that assumes the obligation and becomes the purchaser to the option seller and seller to the option buyer immediately after sale and purchase orders are matched between the option seller and the option buyer.

Out of the Money:
The striking price of the option is above the current market price of the underlying security.

"Out of the Money" Option:
An option whose exercise (striking) price is above the current market price of the underlying security.

Over-the-Counter Option:
An option contract sold in over-the-counter put and call markets.

"Parity" Option:
An option is said to have reached "Parity" when the premium plus the exercise (striking) price equal the market price of the underlying security.

Partial Covered Writing:
Selling (writing) an option contract involving a number of shares that exceeds the number of shares owned.

"Perpendicular" Spread:
A spread involving simultaneous buying and selling of options having the same expiration month but different striking prices. A "perpendicular" spread is sometimes called "money" or "vertical" spread.

"Position One, Sell Two":
An option strategy whereby a ratio writer sells two options against 100 shares of the underlying security held.

Premium:

The price an option buyer pays the option writer (seller) for an option contract.

"Profit Band":

A profit protection zone formed by the upside and downside breakeven points within which a ratio writer will remain profitable so long as the price of the underlying security stays between these two parameters.

Put Option:

An option to sell a specified number of shares of a specific stock at a fixed price, with a specific time period. A put option is a call option in reverse.

Ratio Spreading:

An option strategy whereby a spreader may choose to construct his spreading position by varying the ratio of his "long" and "short" options.

Ratio Writing:

An option strategy whereby an option writer (seller) may choose to partially hedge his position by combining the writing of covered option(s) with that of uncovered option(s) on the same underlying security. Ratio writing is sometimes called "variable" hedging.

Regulation T:

The Federal Reserve Board rule governing, among other things, the amount of credit (if any) that initially may be extended by a broker to his customer.

Return on Cash Flow:

The immediate return on actual dollar commitment, indicating leverage based on cash flow.

Reverse Charge:

Reverse charge is the cost of converting the call portion of a straddle option into a put. This charge is normally smaller than the conversion charge, which is the cost of converting the put portion of a straddle option into a call.

Reverse Horizontal Hedge:

A variation of ratio spreading whereby the spreader buys two near-term options and sells one far-term option having the same striking price.

"Sandwich" Spread:

An option spread consisting of the sale of two intermediate options and the purchase of two options with striking prices of equal distance from the "short" options, in the ratio of 1:2:1. A "sandwich" spread is sometimes called "butterfly."

Secondary Market:

The liquidity, or secondary market capability, of listed options is in sharp contrast to over-the-counter options, which have no liquidity or secondary market-making ability until the expirations of option contracts or until option buyers see fit to exercise their options.

Spread:

A combination option that normally combines a put option at a price below the current market price of the underlying security and a call option at a price above the current market price of the underlying security.

Spread (Bear):
> An option strategy whereby one (1) sells (shorts) the far-term option and buys the near-term option; or (2) sells (shorts) the low-strike option and buys the high-strike option.

Spread (Bull):
> An option strategy whereby one (1) sells (shorts) the near-term option and buys the long-term option; or (2) one sells (shorts) the high-strike option and buys the low-strike option.

Spread "in Credit":
> A spread is said to be in credit when the cost of the "long" option is less than that of the "short" option.

Spread "in Debit":
> A spread is said to be in debit when the cost of the "long" option is more than that of the "short" option.

Spread Premium:
> The differential between buying and selling option premiums.

Standardized Expiration Dates:
> Listed options have standardized expiration dates in sharp contrast to over-the-counter options which can expire on any one of the business days of the year.

Straddle:

An option combining one call and one put written on the same underlying security at the same striking price with the same expiration date.

Striking Price:

The price per unit at which the holder of a listed call option may purchase the underlying security upon exercise. The striking price is sometimes called the "exercise price."

Taking Cover:

A transaction whereby an uncovered (naked) option writer may, during the life of the option, buy the underlying security, thereby becoming a covered writer.

Tangible Value:

The tangible value of a listed call option is the difference between the market value of the underlying security and the exercise (striking) price of the option. Tangible value is sometimes called "intrinsic value."

Three-Against-One Writing:

An option strategy whereby a ratio writer will sell three options against 100 shares of the underlying security held.

"Time" Spread:

A spread involving simultaneous buying and selling of options having the same striking price but different expiration months. A "time" spread is sometimes called "calendar" or "horizontal" spread.

Total Return:

A concept of investment return based on aggregate yields from invested capital from dividends, option premiums, and capital gains earned from option-writing activities.

Two-Against-One Writing:

An option strategy whereby a ratio writer will write two calls against 100 shares of the underlying security held.

Uncovered Writer:

An option writer who does not own the shares or other units of the underlying security covered by the option. An uncovered writer is also called a naked writer.

Uncovered Writing:

Writing (selling) an option, with the writer (seller) owning no shares covered by the option.

Underlying Security:

The security subject to being purchased upon the exercise of an option.

Unit of Trading:

The number of units of the underlying security designated by the Options Clearing Corporation as the subject of a single option. In the absence of any other designation, the unit of trading for common stock is 100 shares.

Upside Parameter:

The upside price level of the underlying security

above which a ratio writer will incur a loss.

Variable Hedging:

An option strategy whereby an option writer (seller) may choose to partially hedge his position by combining the writing of covered option(s) with that of uncovered option(s) on the same underlying security. Variable hedging is sometimes called "ratio" writing.

"Vertical" Spread:

A spread involving simultaneous buying and selling of options having the same expiration month but different striking prices. A "vertical" spread is sometimes called "money" or "perpendicular" spread.

Writer:

The seller of an option contract.

Writing Against Cash:

An uncovered or naked option is written against cash.

OPTIONS QUESTIONNAIRE

On What To Focus

The Options Questionnaire is designed to help the reader know on what to focus in the course of studying the subjects covered by this book.

Question-and-Answer Method

It is suggested the focusing be done by the reader asking himself the following series of salient questions and seeking answers in the course of reading the book.

Considerable Drill

This method of reading with a "focus" appears particularly appropriate for a subject matter such as options that requires considerable drill and exercises to reach deeper layers of option buying, writing, straddling, and spreading techniques, and to uncover their ever-widening interfacing applications.

A.   ON LISTED OPTIONS AND LISTED OPTIONS MARKETS

1. What is the basic difference between options and short-term warrants?
2. What is the basic difference between listed options now traded on the national options exchanges and the traditional options traded over the counter?
3. What accounts for the phenomenal growth of listed options in the last two-plus years since their debut on

the Chicago Board Options Exchange?

4. What are the two major innovations of the listed options market?

5. What are the basic exclusive characteristics of listed options?

6. What accounts for the liquidity of the listed options market?

7. What accounts for the ability of listed options possibly to achieve the two normally irreconcilable objectives of maximizing gains and minimizing risks?

8. What accounts for the risk-limiting characteristics of listed options?

9. What makes listed options small-capital-expenditure vehicles for participation in America's top-quality companies?

10. What is the unique guaranteeing function of the Options Clearing Corporation?

B.   ON OPTION VALUES

11. What is the built-in leverage in option price movements relative to price movements in their underlying securities?

12. What are the general yardsticks to determine the cost or value of options?

13. Is there an intrinsic value for an option?

14. How evaluate "in the money" options and "out of the money" options?

15. How determine the best time-period value of options?

16. Why is the largest option premium percentagewise often paid for the shortest period of time? Why is the option premium for the initial three months higher than the next three-month period? How take advantage of this time-value aberration?

17. How calculate relative overvaluation or undervaluation among options and between options and their underlying securities?
18. Do you need a computer and to be a mathematician to calculate the value of options?
19. What are the principal advantages and disadvantages of computer-based option programs?
20. How salvage option values even if anticipated movement in the underlying security should fail to materialize?
21. Why should you be alert to option opportunities especially during the initial trading hours of a newly listed option?

C.   ON VARIOUS OPTION STRATEGIES

22. What are the basic option strategies?
23. Which of the following is generally considered to be the most speculative?
    (a) Covered writing.
    (b) Uncovered writing.
    (c) Straight "long" stock position.
    (d) Straight option buying.
    (e) Spreading.
    (f) Straddling.
24. What should you do if you believe the price of a stock will rise? Buy a call? Is there any other possible approach, especially if you are in high income bracket and had capital losses?
25. How calculate the potential maximum return and exposure for option buyers?
26. What should you do if you believe the price of a stock will decline? Sell a call? Buy an "in the money" call and sell short the underlying security?

27. What are the relative advantages and disadvantages of the above two approaches?
28. How calculate the potential maximum return and exposure for option writers (sellers)?
29. What should you do if you believe the stock is going to change very little? Buy the stock and sell a call against the stock? Or buy the stock and sell two calls against the stock? What are the relative merits and demerits of these two approaches?
30. What are the most appropriate market conditions for option writing? For option selling? For option straddling? For option spreading?
31. Which of the following is generally considered more likely to make money?
    (a) Writing (selling) options, or
    (b) Buying options.
32. What is your personal opinion as to the comparative profitability of writing (selling) or buying options?

D.   ON OPTION BUYING AND ITS TECHNIQUES

33. What are the principal advantages and disadvantages of option buying?
34. What are the principal call option buying strategies?
35. What are the merits of buying stocks for the purpose of writing call options to obtain additional income?
36. How protect against an upward price movement of a stock that you do not own?
37. How establish a stock position before receiving the expected funds.
38. How buy stocks at below-market prices?
39. How control more stock with the same amount of money?
40. How acquire an option at no cost?

41. How release cash while retaining your market position?
42. How hedge against a short sale?

E. ON OPTION WRITING AND ITS TECHNIQUES

43. What are the principal advantages and disadvantages of option writing (selling)?
44. What are the principal option writing strategies?
45. How increase your cash return while retaining the security?
46. How reduce the cost of the stock that you have acquired?
47. How sell stocks at above-market prices?
48. How do you buy-wait-write?
49. When would it be advantageous for you to write options with a view toward their being called away?
50. How calculate the potential gain from stocks written for options if and when they are called away?
51. How create short-term losses for tax purposes?
52. What are the possible recourses for protecting your uncovered position?

F. ON RATIO WRITING AND ITS TECHNIQUES

53. What are the principal advantages and disadvantages of ratio writing or variable hedging?
54. How calculate the potential maximum return and exposure for ratio writers?
55. How establish a profit band in ratio writing?
56. How calculate the downside parameter for ratio writing?
57. How calculate the upside parameter for ratio writing?
58. What are the principal ratio writing strategies?

59. How set up a 2-against-1 ratio writing?
60. How set up a 3-against-1 ratio writing?
61. How buy at discount instead of premium?

G.   ON OPTION SPREADING AND ITS TECHNIQUES

62. What are the principal advantages and disadvantages of option spreading?
63. How select stocks for spreads?
64. What are the principal option spreading strategies?
65. How calculate the potential maximum return and exposure for option spreaders?
66. How balance downside protection with upside potential in option spreading?
67. How set up a bull "horizontal" ("time" or "calendar") spread? And a bear "horizontal" spread?
68. How set up a bull "vertical" ("money" or "perpendicular") spread? And a bear "vertical" spread?
69. How establish a higher-potential spread position at reduced risk?
70. How buy below-intrinsic-value options?

H.   ON OPTION STRADDLING AND ITS TECHNIQUES

71. How make money without knowing market directions?
72. What is the principal difference between a straddle and a spread?
73. Why is a straddle generally more expensive than a spread, a put, or a call?
74. Why are volatile stocks more desirable for straddling?
75. What are the principal straddle option writing strategies?
76. How sell a straddle without a stock position?
77. How offset a "short" position with a straddle?

78. How convert two calls into a put and a call?
79. How recoup the entire straddle premium with only half the option?
80. How achieve profit pyramiding?

I.   ON PUT OPTION AND ITS TECHNIQUES

81. What are the principal advantages and disadvantages of put options?
82. What are the principal put option strategies?
83. What is the basic difference between a put option and a short sale?
84. What is the basic difference between a put option and a buy-stop?
85. How insulate short-term market breaks?
86. How profit from down fluctuations?

J.   ON OPTION MARGINS

87. What are the three sets of option margin requirements?
88. What is the difference between the initial margin requirement and the maintenance margin requirement?
89. What is the margin requirement (if any) for covered writing?
90. How calculate the margin requirement for uncovered or naked writing?
91. How calculate the margin requirement for ratio or variable writing?
92. What are the improved margin advantages for spreading?
93. How minimize the cost of spreading?
94. What are the main differences between bull spread margins and bear spread margins?

95. What are the basic tax considerations for option buyers?
96. How realize a long-term gain on decline?
97. How realize a long-term gain on rise?
98. What are the basic tax considerations for option writers?
99. How convert a short-term to a long-term gain?
100. How create ordinary loss with an offsetting option? With an offsetting stock?
101. If an option writer's obligation is closed by executing a closing purchase transaction, what is the Internal Revenue Service's rule on tax treatment of profits from option writing?
102. If an option is exercised, what is the Internal Revenue Service's rule on tax treatment of an option premium received?
103. If an option expires unexercised, what is the Internal Revenue Service's rule on tax treatment of an option premium received?
104. What are the special tax advantages for straddle writing?
105. What are the most frequently used option techniques for tax-shelter purposes?

L.   ON OPTION PORTFOLIOS?

106. What are the principal means of increasing the yield for an income-oriented portfolio using options?
107. What would be the most appropriate option programs for conservative accounts whose portfolios are composed primarily of low-cost, quality stocks?
108. What are the alternate income-oriented option

strategies for option-oriented portfolios?

109. What are the possible obstacles to reaching maximum yields achievable through income-oriented strategies?

110. What would be the most appropriate portfolio composition for income-oriented accounts in terms of percentage allocation among writing, buying, and spreading segments?

111. What are the principal means of maximizing gains for a growth-oriented portfolio, using options?

112. What would be the most appropriate options programs for aggressive accounts primarily seeking capital appreciation?

113. What are the possible obstacles to reaching the maximum gains achievable through aggressive strategies?

114. What would be the most appropriate portfolio composition for growth-oriented accounts in terms of percentage allocation among writing, buying, and spreading segments?

115. What are the principal means of maximizing gains for a balanced (income and growth) portfolio, using options?

116. What would be the most appropriate portfolio composition for balanced accounts in terms of percentage allocation among writing, buying, and spreading segments?

Lin Tso, a veteran securities analyst in special situations, is the author of four widely read books on the stock market: The Investor's Guide to Stock Market Profits in Seasoned and Emerging Industries (1969), Techniques For Discovering Hidden Value Stocks (1965), The Sensible Investor's Guide To Growth Stocks (1961), and How the Experts Buy Stocks For Profits (1960).

Mr. Tso was educated both in China and in the United States, including graduate work at The John Hopkins University. In addition to being a financial consultant, Mr. Tso also writes for investment research organizations, including regular option market letters on listed options.